Revenue makes you
VISIBLE.

Profit makes you
POWERFUL.

Staying true to
yourself makes you
UNSTOPPABLE.

THE HONORABLE
Entrepreneur

PHILIPP BAASKE

Disclaimer

This memoir reflects the author's present recollections of events. Some names, roles, and identifying details have been changed; certain scenes and dialogue have been reconstructed from memory, and where necessary, timelines have been compressed for narrative clarity. The memoir is offered for informational and reflective purposes only and does not constitute legal, financial, or professional advice.

Cover design by: U.T., 99D
Cover photo by: Stefan Schmerold / blende11 Fotografen
Book design by: SWATT Books Ltd

Printed in the United Kingdom
First Printing, 2025

ISBN: 978-3-9827695-0-9 (Paperback)
ISBN: 978-3-9827695-1-6 (eBook)

Philipp Baaske
81379 Muenchen
Germany

www.philippbaaske.com

CONTENTS

PHILIPP BAASKE

INTRODUCTION: THE HONORABLE ENTREPRENEUR

The email came in on a quiet Sunday evening. It was the kind of message every entrepreneur dreams of receiving – an acquisition offer.

The number was so large and the screen so small that I had to zoom in, then zoom out again. Hundreds of millions. A life-changing figure.

I put my iPhone down. My hands were cold. I walked to the window – I needed time to think. I should have felt excitement, relief even. But I just stood there, shivering.

If I were to say yes, everything would change. Everything. The company I had created. The people who had trusted me. The mission that had driven me.

For years, I had fought to stay independent – to prove that scaling fast and staying profitable weren't mutually exclusive. And now? I had two options... To take the money and walk away. Or to bet on myself one more time.

It was a peak of a biotech boom. Private equity firms and global corporations were circling. They wanted to buy NanoTemper, the company I had built from scratch.

The offers were massive – hundreds of millions. I could have cashed out and moved on. But I couldn't shake off one important question: what would happen after I had sold?

I pictured myself sitting across from financial investors – watching them optimize for short-term returns, cutting R&D to hit next quarter's numbers at the expense of long-term vision, prioritizing spreadsheets over real impact, and sacrificing our purpose. That made my stomach turn.

I wasn't about to hand over my life's work to someone who saw it as just another asset.

It wasn't an easy decision: there was no playbook for this moment, no guide, and no one to tell me what to do. Just sleepless nights and red eyes.

It prompted me to dig deep and ask myself important questions. What did I want to achieve? What made me satisfied? What made me happy?

Did this involve financial indicators, such as revenue or profit? Was it wealth? Would I be truly happy if I became a multi-millionaire or even a billionaire?

I had to choose the harder path, so I turned the offer down. Later, I realized that the path was one I'd been following all along – but without knowing it had a name: the path of the Honorable Entrepreneur.

The founder's dilemma

You might be thinking: "Why didn't you take the money?"

You'd be forgiven for thinking that money makes you happy. Especially when you read success stories in the media about hundred-million-dollar funding rounds and founders selling their companies. All those smiling faces in the press releases.

When you raise this kind of funding, you'll be a rockstar for a week. For sure, you'll be very happy. But will this happiness stand the test of time? When your shareholders force you to attend a quarterly meeting on the day of your daughter's birthday? I've seen too many founders sacrifice their families and their health just for money.

When you sell your company for a billion dollars, you'll become a superstar of your industry. Everyone will know you. You will have the freedom to buy whatever you want: the dream house, the Ferrari, the first-class holidays.

I've met many founders who have been immediately happy after selling their company. But after a while, once the noise dies down and they've bought everything they ever dreamed of, a different question starts to trouble them: is this it? The happiness has gone by then...

I've heard this quiet regret in every private meeting I've ever had with one of those founders. Such as Marion, who told me at the inauguration party for our new headquarters in Munich that "Selling our company was a mistake. We should have kept it and enjoyed it ourselves." Even in the US, CEOs urge me "Philipp, if you can keep your independence, keep it. Sacrificing it is not worth the money."

You often see founders starting a new business similar to the one they've already sold. They're not happy about what happened to their legacy, so they begin from scratch, all over again.

Why I didn't sell NanoTemper

When, after two decades in business, I started to uncover what made me happy, I realized that staying true to my values was key – every day, now as well as in the future.

That's why I didn't sell NanoTemper.

After listening to the stories, I saw a pattern. Deep down, I knew I would become one more of those founders. Yes, I would be rich. Maybe even famous. But I would regret it, possibly every single day.

I knew that NanoTemper still had so much potential. Our brilliant team was the reason we could achieve our mission, and I didn't want to hand all that over to someone else. What's more, why sell NanoTemper for several hundred million dollars now, knowing that we might earn such a figure annually in a few years?

Not selling wasn't an easy decision. I didn't speak about it, because I thought everyone would call me crazy. But I wasn't building the company to sell it – I was building it to create something lasting.

I was following a different kind of entrepreneurial path as well as a different way of doing business. That decision – that Sunday evening – was a final moment of clear understanding. It was also the moment when this book began...

This is the guide that I wish I'd had at the time: a blueprint for building a business that lasts – as well as a life you won't want to walk away from.

THE CODE OF HONOR

At the heart of this book lies what I call the "Honorable Entrepreneur's Code of Honor" – a set of principles shaping not only how we build companies, but also who we become as leaders.

These aren't simply values. No, they constitute the very framework that can make such a path possible. Together, they offer a battle-tested foundation that has guided me – and that can guide you, too.

Each chapter in this book comes back to these core commitments...

I build trust – or I build nothing
Trust is the foundation of each and every business. If people can't trust me, they won't follow me. I will communicate openly, act with integrity, and deliver on my commitments: **a promise made is a promise kept.**

I put people first – always
Business is about people, not just numbers. I will pay good salaries and lead with fairness, loyalty, and respect – empowering my team, valuing diversity, and **building a culture where people do their best work.** The strongest companies are built by the strongest teams.

I innovate for impact
Innovation isn't about making noise – it's about solving real problems. I won't create technology for the sake of it: I will build solutions that move industries forward, make a difference, and stand the test of time.

I scale smart and fast
Speed wins, but recklessness kills. I will grow with discipline, making bold moves without burning resources or credibility. Scaling is not only about getting bigger, it's also about getting stronger, smarter, and more impactful.

I build a profitable business that lasts

Profitability isn't optional: it's the foundation of long-term success. A strong business is financially independent, sustainable, and built for the future – with more than just a final exit in mind. I will focus on growth with discipline and resilience.

I execute my vision

Ideas are worthless without action. I won't just talk – I will build, sell, ship, and adapt. I will take bold steps, minimize unnecessary risks, and turn vision into reality – because execution separates the dreamers from the builders.

I give back

Success isn't just about what I build for myself – it's also about how many others I help build. I will mentor, fund, and create opportunities for the next generation of entrepreneurs. A winner takes the prize. A leader passes the torch.

This isn't just a list of rules – it's a framework for scaling with integrity, growing fast while staying in control, and winning without losing your soul.

This book is for:

- founders who want to build, scale, and sustain great companies – without selling out;
- deep-tech and biotech entrepreneurs who are balancing scientific progress with commercial success; and
- leaders who want to create a business that lasts for decades – not just look for an exit.

The Honorable Entrepreneur isn't just a business model – it's a mindset shift: a commitment to scaling without shortcuts, growing with integrity, and staying true to your mission.

LET'S BUILD TOGETHER

This is my story. More importantly, though, it's also *your path forward*.

I built NanoTemper into a business doing 56 million euros per year from scratch. I've had moments of near-failure. I've made tough decisions. I've broken rules.

I know what it's like to bet everything on an idea. To wake up at 3:00 a.m. questioning every decision. To wonder if you're building something great – or whether you're just insane. I've been there! And if you've made it this far, I know you've been there too.

That's why this book isn't just about what I've built – it's about *what you'll build next*.

If you've ever felt that scaling fast while staying independent wasn't possible, this book will prove otherwise.

Let's do this. Let's build a community. And let's start a new era of entrepreneurship – together...

PHILIPP BAASKE

1: THE AWAKENING – FROM SCIENTIST TO FOUNDER

I started out as a scientist, focusing purely on research, but life had other plans for me. An internship at a biotech startup showed me the power of purpose-driven innovation. A "bad" career decision took me to Munich, where I met my co-founder Stefan Duhr and discovered the magic of teamwork. And a deeply personal event – my mother's cancer diagnosis – gave me my why for biotech.

BAD AND GOOD CAREER DECISIONS

"Can you please donate your sperm?" asked Tanja. I was a 24-year-old student, and this was my first exposure to biotechnology. At first, I didn't understand. Then I blushed a deep crimson red.

This was in 2003, at Alopex, in Kulmbach – a place that is known as the "secret capital of beer brewing." Alopex's vision was to transform testing for successful in vitro fertilization. They concentrated on examining tiny structures called polar bodies, which are linked to egg cells, to check whether each egg had the correct – and therefore healthy – number of chromosomes. This matters, because when that number's off, it can lead to serious conditions – such as Down syndrome, where an extra chromosome 21 leads to developmental and intellectual delays, or

Edwards' syndrome, which causes severe complications and often results in early infant death.

Polar bodies are scarce – after all, fertilization requires two parties – so we started looking at the other contributor of chromosomes: male sperm cells. And, as we all know, with the right motivation, one can obtain infinite amounts of those. My motivation? Let's call it science. I've never come across restrooms that well equipped since...

As an intern at Alopex, while studying for my degree, I experienced the startup feeling for the very first time: great people, low pay, 12-hour days, and failing 91% of the time – while somehow still also having fun. We enjoyed ourselves because we had a strong motivation: to help people who are suffering. We can all appreciate that an unfulfilled desire for a child can cause immense suffering, and everyone knows someone who has faced this deeply emotional issue. It can destroy relationships, plans, and dreams. Improving the lives of these people was the motivation that drove us forward.

This startup experience shaped my life profoundly: I was only there for a few months, yet it had a massive impact on me. It anchored the concepts of founders, startups, and entrepreneurship in my mind. I loved the startup spirit and also the people who shared this mindset. I'm still in touch with Tanja, who asked me that strange first question about donating my sperm. And I'm still in touch with Thomas, the cool physicist from Hamburg who mentored me during my time there. 12 years later, he helped me again – via his new role at Hamilton Robotics – with the automation of our NanoTemper instruments. When I strongly connect with people, I connect with them forever.

Not long after that first startup experience, I faced another critical choice: knowing that I would finish my studies in biophysics in July 2005, I had to decide where I was going to pursue my PhD. Everyone in science knows how important this choice is for a later career in academia.

Initially, I had two options:

1. to stay where I was – my good old *alma mater*, the University of Bayreuth; or
2. to move to Göttingen, to do my PhD in the lab of Stefan W. Hell, a renowned professor at the Max Planck Institute (MPI) and a prominent figure in biophysics.

At 26, having been born and raised in the rural region north of Bayreuth, it was now time to move on. Göttingen, then, seemed to be the obvious choice. One day, however, a third opportunity appeared...

A casually dressed junior research leader visited our lab in Bayreuth. Wearing corduroy pants and a worn-out white t-shirt, Dieter had intense eyes – like an X-ray, always looking through you – as well as a winning smile.

A couple of factors suggested that following this route would be a bad idea. First, he was looking for PhD students willing to work for 1,400 euros per month in Munich – an expensive city. Second, there was zero probability that I'd achieve high-impact scientific publications from this research topic, meaning it would be a bad choice for a scientific career.

Even so, the research topic – "the origin of life" – was exciting! Ever since I read Goethe's *Faust*, I had been dreaming about discovering "what makes the world go round." Wasn't this in fact the perfect topic for me?

What's more, Dieter had such a high energy level, and it was obvious that I could learn a lot from him. After just two meetings, he convinced me to join his group in Munich at Ludwig-Maximilians-University (LMU). We agreed on the main research topic for my PhD – "The Origin of Life, Experimental

Biophysics, and Enzyme-free Replication of RNA (Ribonucleic Acid)" – and we agreed that I'd start in Munich at the beginning of October. I guess, at that relatively young age, I wasn't aware of my craziness!

On 4 October 2005, at precisely 8:27 a.m., I knocked on the closed wooden door of Dieter's office a little early. Nothing. Knock, knock. Again, a good sound – but still nothing. No response at all. I stood alone before a closed door, a small-town boy in a big new city. Maybe I was too early?

At around 9:03 a.m., when I was losing all my patience, a PhD student from a neighboring research group encountered me. Immediately understanding that I was lost, he informed me that Dieter and his group were in the nearby mountains, on a hiking tour. "Must have forgotten you," he added. "Espresso?" "Oh, yes," I replied. At least the coffee was good!

Forgotten by my supervisor on my first day of work, I promised myself that I would learn from this – but that onboarding experience set the tone for my entire PhD. In the nearly five years that followed, nothing I attempted for my main scientific project ended up working. I had failed at science! You could call this an especially bad decision after Professor Stefan W. Hell, whose job offer I had turned down, was awarded the Nobel Prize for Chemistry in 2014, after inventing super-resolution STED microscopy.

Dieter, however, remains one of the brightest scientific minds I've ever met. And while my decision may have been bad for my scientific career, it did lead me to Stefan Duhr, who became my co-founder at NanoTemper.

FROM PUBLISHING TO INVENTING

Dieter headed an independent Emmy Noether research group. Having secured a grant for only a limited period of time, he was aiming for a professorship, and he had to publish to achieve this.

There were three important things for our group, then:

1. publish;
2. publish some more; and
3. publish with high impact.

This was a lot of pressure for all of us! Dieter tried to maximize our output by having us work in parallel on different projects. This meant that there was no teamwork in our group. Stefan, Franz (another colleague), and I worked on separate projects. Only then did I realize that I wasn't a one-man show and that I don't work well alone.

Later, our entire department went skiing for two days in the nearby mountains – the Munich Alps. Everyone was excited and talking about it for weeks – both the location as well as the après-ski parties. Over 30 undergrads, PhD students, postdocs, and professors set off for the Alps, leaving the building empty and quiet. Everyone? Well, not quite... Stefan and I stayed behind in the lab.

We had developed a joint idea for a secret research project: "Melting Curve Analysis in a Snapshot." We knew that if we could promise a fast publication, Dieter wouldn't stop us.

We had the lab to ourselves and focused completely on our work. I was gluing microfluidic chambers made of plastic and glass – hundreds of them – with nail polish like crazy. Stefan was preparing the samples. It was productive teamwork. A high-power 5-watt infrared (IR) laser was focused on the sample in the chamber. Two seconds of measurement, before a quick look at the imaging data, then onto the next experiment.

We started in the morning and didn't stop until the evening: gluing, samples, IR laser experiments, image analysis, then through the whole process again. It was teamwork, but it was hard work. Tired, with blurry eyes and headaches, we finally achieved the breakthrough, identifying single-point mutations in DNA 10,000 times faster than the existing state-of-the-art technologies. Our measurement took 50 milliseconds, while the other technologies needed nearly 10 minutes to complete this so-called melting curve analysis.

The teamwork, as well as the extra effort, made us successful. The combination of Stefan's biochemistry skills with my biophysics perspective proved key to our innovation. While everyone else was enjoying the skiing, we executed our idea. Going the extra mile – putting in more effort than others – is often part of the straightforward yet challenging journey to success. Dieter didn't reject this project, which was published in *Applied Physics* at record speed.

However, after nearly two years of research – two years of Big Bang theory in reality and two years of being blinded by the light of fancy high-power laser experiments – I realized one day that research was not my thing. I'd never become a good scientist!

At this time, after more than 4,000 hours in the lab, my eyes had finally opened to the fact that I had never considered "why" something is as it is. Rather, my focus had always been on "what" I could do with it. What is this good for? (Absolutely nothing? Hopefully this is not always the answer…) What real problem can I solve through application? In other words, I had finally realized that applying a technology excites me much more than understanding the science behind it.

I am not someone who quits, though. I had a clear plan for completing my PhD and had just started thinking about what to do afterward. Science was off the table, so what else was there?

Many of the students in our department ended up becoming patent attorneys or business consultants. BCG and McKinsey were just down the road in Munich Schwabing. As a consultant, you see a lot, learn a lot, and earn good money.

I'd heard that admission was competitive. They only select the best candidates. Therefore, I was considering ways to enhance my CV. Scientific publications aren't always helpful. Perhaps having patents would be more beneficial? Especially since Stefan and I had just invented a new measurement method.

I had no idea how to write a patent, so I asked for assistance from a network of German biotech students. I emailed their network: "Who knows how to write a patent for a biophysical measurement method?"

An unknown man named Lars responded to my email in an unexpected manner: "I don't know how to write a patent, but I work at the Entrepreneurial Center of the LMU and I am supervising a Business Plan seminar for economics students. Your inventions have potential for developing a business plan about them."

A business plan? I'd never even thought about one... That's even better for the CV than a patent. Yes, let's do it, absolutely!

We accepted Lars' offer and participated in his Business Plan seminar. It was quite successful: on 24 July 2007, our university published the following press release:

NanoTemper Technologies

The team composed of young researchers from the Braun group at the Gaub chair (LMU) has already won prizes in the first ("ideas stage") and second round ("development stage") of the competition. They are assisted by Marco Hierling, a student in business administration. Yesterday, Philipp Baaske and Dr. Stefan Duhr were awarded a prize of 5,000 Euro for finishing third in the so-called "Sprinter"-section of the final round ("excellence stage") with their business idea to use their novel measuring technique for the fast characterization of biomolecules. This technology has broad applications for biotechnological research and medical diagnostics.

This success and all the feedback we received caused us to change our plan: it was no longer about pimping a CV but instead about business – about founding a startup. We immediately trademarked "NanoTemper" as the brand name. A good start for a business! We thought we had everything we needed to move forward...

But one person reading the press release had thought ahead and managed to sabotage us, by registering the domain name "www.nanotemper.com" for himself, before we had done so. He was motivated by a desire to one-up Professor Gaub, under whose chair we worked, because he had had a private fight with him. We didn't know this person and we didn't know about his completely unrelated issue with Professor Gaub. Of course, we'd been naïve not to register the domain name before publishing the press release. But even so, how crazy is that?!

You cannot prepare for this. Over the coming years, we had to learn one thing the hard way: there are evil people out there, who become interested in you when they sense the potential for big money.

I soon learned that founders must build a strong team. Problems and temptations will arise, plus conflicts will occur. You need to develop mechanisms to address these issues. Otherwise, you may jeopardize your efforts. Many startups fail because founders engage in conflicts they cannot resolve, blocking each other and ultimately destroying their company. Trust me – no matter how good things seem at the time, conflicts will happen, sooner or later! If you can't develop a mechanism to deal with your conflicts, seek help from someone you deeply trust or from external coaches and mentors. This can become a game-changer for you!

You may have noticed that the narrative has started to move from "I" to "we." Stefan Duhr and I formed a very strong relationship, to the extent that our wives say that we are somehow married to each other. Of course, we have had conflicts – with each other and, even more, with the systems and structures surrounding us. There is some wisdom in the phrase that "every problem you solve makes you stronger." This has been very true for us and our relationship.

Speaking of conflicts – founding a company while doing a PhD is a conflict in itself. Your supervisor cares about science and publications. Your focus – inevitably – drifts toward your startup. And, let's be honest, the relationship between a PhD student and a supervisor is already a complicated one. Now add "co-founder and CEO of a biotech startup" into the mix and you're heightening the pressure considerably.

My supervisor and I clashed – often. Dieter urgently needed publications to advance his career, as he hadn't yet secured a professorship. His role was to push for papers. Mine, as a PhD student, was to deliver them. But in my second role – as one of the founders of NanoTemper – scientific papers weren't a priority. Obtaining funding and finding customers were. That created a serious challenge, especially because we all shared the same open office and lab space – all of Dieter's PhD students and all of NanoTemper's early team. For me, there was no way to separate my two roles. Not physically. Not mentally. I felt torn –sometimes even torn apart.

Two things kept me from being worn down completely. My strong bond with Stefan, my co-founder. And a more personal reason: my family – or my why.

MY WHY

By 2006, I had adapted to and was much enjoying life in the big city of Munich. Our lab was located at the heart of the vibrant center known as "Schwabing." It felt like there were a hundred pubs within a 500-meter radius of our workplace, providing plenty of opportunities for a beer after our typical 12-hour working day. Work hard, party hard – there is some truth to that...

The architecture of the 1972 Olympic Stadium continues to attract many superstars to Munich. One Friday evening, I enjoyed a Bon Jovi concert there. The following Saturday, I drove to my home village of Kirchleus, to visit my parents. As you might imagine, I was in a good mood. My parents, as always, greeted me at the door to the house.

Me: "Munich is so great. Bon Jovi rocked it yesterday!"
My mother: "I have breast cancer..."

The words from the song "It's My Life" came pulsating through while everything stood still for a moment. Then my world fell apart. My mother was only 51 years old at the time: I had thought that she was going to live forever.

I felt a deep shock. And I was speechless – there are no right words to say at such a moment. Then I gave in to my feelings, embracing my mom, crying while holding her tightly. I'd already lost my grandmother and my youngest uncle to cancer. She proceeded to tell me that she had a severe form of breast cancer. I'd never felt so powerless. It was devastating.

Then my new hero stepped in to play a part: biotechnology. Or, more precisely, Herceptin (Trastuzumab), an antibody developed by the biotechnology company Genentech, based in San Francisco (and part of the Swiss Roche concern). This biotech-based drug saved my mother's life and changed my own life as well.

This is my why – why I am in biotech. It gives us hope. My entire family suffers from cancer, and I too have a high probability of developing it. That said, it is not just about me and my family. There are 18 million new cancer cases worldwide each year, and every one is one too many. This was my call to duty: I didn't want to be a victim of fate.

I asked myself: "What can I do to fight cancer? Develop a drug against it? A drug like Trastuzumab?" This was not my area of expertise. It would also be a multi-year and multi-billion bet, with a low probability of succeeding. So what could I do?

Slowly, an idea about using optical tools for drug development started to materialize in my mind. How could I make the biggest impact? What if I could support scientists with better tools and instruments in order to develop new and improved drugs? Would this enable them to create lifesaving therapies more quickly?

That is why I founded NanoTemper: to make the invisible visible by means of biophysical tools, allowing scientists to drug the previously undruggable.

Spoiler alert: I now feel very proud, as more than 10,000 scientists, engineers, and developers are using our biophysical tools for drug discovery and development. My first mission has been accomplished!

SUMMARY

MY PERSONAL SHIFT MOMENT

From uncovering what I wasn't good at to discovering my why, the years from 2003 to 2007 shaped everything that followed. I stopped being a curious biophysics student and started being a startup founder, with a mission that had nothing to do with getting rich and everything to do with making an impact.

- At Alopex, I was immersed in startup life for the first time, with chaos, creativity, and mission-driven founders – it felt like home.

- I made what looked like a terrible career decision, turning down a future Nobel laureate in order to follow my vision – but that decision turned out to be the best one of my life.

- I learned that I'd never become the great scientist I had wanted to become, finding instead that my talent involved transforming scientific knowledge into usable products.

- When my mother was diagnosed with breast cancer, biotech saved her life – that changed everything and proved to be my call to duty.

It was during this period that the idea of founding a company first took root: not as a path to money or status, but as a means of fighting diseases like cancer. To help find better therapies – and faster. It was my path to creating a fulfilled and meaningful life.

How this chapter lives the Code of Honor

I build trust – or I build nothing

My mother entrusted her life to a biotech drug – and it saved her. That moment taught me that if scientists trust me to build tools that can accelerate their discoveries, I must never let them down. Trust is earned, and it's everything.

I put people first – always

I wasn't a lone wolf, and I never wanted to be one. Teaming up with Stefan, a biochemist with a totally different personality, proved to be a game-changer for me. That partnership developed into a bond so strong that our wives say we're practically married. Innovation was the outcome, but trust and loyalty were the foundation.

I innovate for impact

At Alopex, I saw that real innovation occurs when science meets suffering. Helping couples struggling with infertility wasn't theoretical – it was responding to an urgent need. That's when I learned that true innovation solves human pain, not merely technical puzzles.

I execute my vision

I didn't wait for permission. Stefan and I pursued an unproven idea in secret, built a prototype in a deserted lab, and turned it into a publication, a patent, and eventually a business. Vision without action is just dreaming – I chose to build.

NOW OVER TO YOU

Don't optimize for money, prestige, or titles. Start with a reason and let your vision guide you. Don't build your company with an exit in mind – build it for your people, for your customers. Because when your work truly matters to others, success will follow.

CHALLENGE FOR YOU

What drives you? What's your vision, your big dream? Write down your why in one short sentence.

2: FIGHTING FOR SURVIVAL – BUILDING AND PROTECTING A STARTUP

We had the technology and the vision, but none of that mattered when we almost lost everything. A Swiss business disaster nearly ended NanoTemper before it had even begun. The 2008 financial crisis caused funding to dry up, forcing us to become resourceful. One hard truth became clear: selling is more important than developing.

YOUR ENVIRONMENT SHAPES YOU

NanoTemper is a spin-off from the Center of NanoScience (CeNS). We were very fortunate with the entrepreneurial spirit at CeNS, with companies being founded both before and after us – such as Nanion, attocube, ibidi, GNA Biosolutions, and Chromotek, to name only a few. Our professors strongly supported this spirit, exposing us to startups nearly every day – something that inevitably shaped our own development. We loved their spirit, so when we had the opportunity to found our own business, we jumped!

During our first few months, we were easily able to ask other founders about their experiences. They were always happy to assist us. In particular, Niels from Nanion was a great help, being five years ahead on his business journey.

"Hey Niels, how did you enter the Japanese market?" we asked. "We worked with Quantum Design Japan," Niels replied. We followed that advice.

"Hey Niels, how do you set up your supply chain and production?" we asked. "Just come by and visit us – you'll see," he replied.

We learned the most from the people who were a few years ahead of us. They were not too far ahead, so they were able to recall their experiences in detail. Because of this, I want to give back now.

We weren't the only CeNS success stories, however. In the last chapter, I mentioned Lars, who invited us to the Business Plan seminar, as well as Marco, the economics student who supported us in writing that business plan. Both have since become successful entrepreneurs, too.

Lars co-founded a biotech company two years after us, in the very same building. He developed fast point-of-care PCR cyclers and sold his company to Hewlett Packard during the Covid pandemic – a time when it must have commanded an impressive price. Marco founded a startup backed by venture capital (VC) and focused on the pet market. It is now a fast-growing holding company and, as the founder and CEO, Marco is acquiring company after company. Hopefully he will also share his experiences in a book.

What we experienced at CeNS is comparable to environments such as the Bay area, the Boston area, and the UK triangle comprising Cambridge, London, and Oxford: there are so many entrepreneurs around you that you run into one whenever you go. When this density of entrepreneurs and supportive institutions reaches a critical mass, it becomes a self-sustaining system. Entrepreneurs attract money, and money attracts entrepreneurs – as well as more money.

When you expose yourself to such an environment, opportunities will arise. You just need to follow one and put it into action.

OWN YOUR INTELLECTUAL PROPERTY

When your business relies on knowledge, technology, or invention, patents are very helpful for protection. Additionally, patents create value, and investors appreciate a strong intellectual property (IP) portfolio.

A patent application, even an international application at the World Intellectual Property Organization, is not expensive. This means that securing the priority of your invention is affordable. The higher costs for the national phases and for maintaining it will come later. With a good attorney, and by writing much of it in advance, the expense amounts to just a few thousand euros. That is mostly worth it. We didn't have ChatGPT or similar tools back then. It must be even easier, now...

We came up with our two inventions and the resulting two patents as PhD students employed by our university. In such a case, German law states that your university can claim the invention. With the first patent application, we followed our university's standard procedure, submitting our first "invention disclosure" in May 2006, with the university claiming it in the late summer.

We had planned our first patent to contain only our "Melting Curve in a Snapshot" idea. As PhD students, however, we had to publish in scientific journals – you can't patent something that you've published before, though, and Stefan was on the verge of publishing a paper on his "Theory of Thermophoresis." Shortly before the publication date, we changed our minds and decided that Thermophoresis would also be included in the patent. It was the best decision ever. However, we had very little time: we had to file the patent in November, before the scientific paper was published in early December (we didn't know the exact publication date).

Thus, in an intense operation – and with substantial support from four patent attorneys at Vossius & Partner – we finalized and submitted our patent application, which was more than a hundred A4 pages in length, just in time. Right before our deadline, I was editing some of the patent's 39 technical sketches one long night. At 4:00 a.m., I had a Glenfiddich – which was a bad idea: some say that one of my later drawings contains a mistake. This first patent is called "Fast Thermo-optical Particle Characterization." We pinned the US certificate to our wall as soon as we received it – again, a very proud moment.

As previously mentioned, we submitted this first patent application in the official manner requested by our university – starting with an "invention disclosure," then waiting for the patent office to decide whether to authorize it, after careful consideration. This worked well, but the process took several months.

Indeed, we got into some trouble with our second patent application, "Thermo-optical Characterization of Nucleic Acid Molecules" – a competitor put us under pressure, so we had to act quickly. We simply didn't have the time to involve the patent office and follow the slow standard procedure. Therefore, we submitted this patent application in the name of our university, without permission, massively overstepping our competencies as PhD students. We received harsh criticism for this. However, we accomplished our most important goal: protecting our IP. In the end, it was good that we took this risk and acted against the rules. Additionally, we were fortunate that Sonja from the patent office was incredibly supportive, investing significantly more time with us than she was compensated for. We remain good friends today.

We now had two international patent applications protecting our methods, applications, and various optical setups. Our knowledge was protected, but we didn't own it. We had to negotiate a contract with the LMU patent office, which was a tough and nerve-wracking thing to do. When you hear founders complaining about their *alma mater*, it is often due to IP transfers.

We had no idea how to negotiate this, so we looked for counsel. Christoph, head of the university's spin-off and technology transfer department, helped us to find Klaus, an experienced advisor. Klaus had previously negotiated an IP transfer contract with LMU shortly before, so he was able to refer to the conditions that he had secured in that contract, which made a significant difference for us. Even so, it still took a long time and a lot of energy to finalize everything.

In the end, we secured a fair contract. It was a global exclusive license, which involved us agreeing to pay license fees for each product we sell that is based on the specified IP portfolio. We negotiated rigorously to include a clause allowing us to subsequently purchase and thus own the IP portfolio. Additionally, we pre-determined the price of the full purchase, ensuring that the university covered all of its costs and made at least a small profit. The university included a "Golden Nugget" clause: if we were to make millions of euros within the first few years, we would be required to pay a significant additional amount to fully own the IP.

We've activated the clause to fully buy and own the IP at the earliest possible date. Our understanding is that it is best to fully own the IP, to have it completely under our control.

No one has copied us yet. But who knows what would have happened if our IP hadn't been protected in this way?

"YOU WILL FAIL, BECAUSE I FAILED"

When you've never started a business before, everything can feel challenging – not just IP! You have a lot to learn. Biotech, AI, and all deep-tech ventures are complex. We needed guidance in all areas – the best guidance we could get.

In 2007, we approached one of the most famous German biotech founders – a successful serial entrepreneur. You could call him the Steve Jobs of German biotech. Fortunately, he was willing to listen to us. He welcomed us at the upscale Four Seasons hotel in Munich, where he was seated in an old-fashioned wooden chair, with a fireplace crackling away in the background. The entire room had a colonial style. He was literally elevated above us.

We pitched our idea and business concept. Then there was silence... Eventually he said "You will fail. You will definitely fail." It was shocking... This experienced and famous entrepreneur was telling us that we wouldn't succeed. He continued: "You will fail because I've already tried what you want to do. It didn't work for me, so it can't work at all."

We left with a bad feeling. When we met the next day, that feeling lingered – yet somehow we still had faith in our idea. We were very confident that it would succeed.

Here's the thing: experienced people are nearly always right about the past, but they can't predict the future. This serial entrepreneur was correct. 15 years ago, the idea couldn't have worked. However, time and technology had changed since then. Because of the explosion of optical internet communications from 1990 to 2006, the IR laser we needed had become very good and affordable. And this is what he didn't have when he tried.

We've learned this: gather as much advice as possible, but also continue to execute your vision – after all, you know it best.

So, was the NanoTemper story a straight line to success? No! Absolutely not! We did fail at the very beginning. In fact, we failed massively...

THE SWISS DISASTER

You may know that NanoTemper Technologies GmbH was founded on 27 May 2008 in Munich.

But have you heard about NanoTemper Technologies AG (NTTAG), which was founded on 10 October 2007 in Baar, Switzerland? No? Well, we're happy that you haven't. Until now, that is...

NTTAG was our first startup, and it failed. It almost ruined my friendship with Stefan, jeopardized my scientific career, affected my personal finances, and disrupted our lives.

Remember when I talked about evil people – evil people who smell big money? I had one of those in my extended family: a 60-year-old with nearly white hair, glasses, and a paunch, who was experienced and also very charming. He drove us in his Porsche to an all-you-can-eat prawn restaurant in Switzerland. This was impressive for PhD students who were only earning 1,400 euros per month!

He convinced us to establish NTTAG with him in Baar, Kanton Zug, Switzerland – famous for its low taxes. We invested all our personal money as well as all our patents. We gave him 34% of the shares, based on nothing but his promises that we would all become rich. I still can't believe we did this. Maybe he was just too clever for us, and we were too naïve in believing his promises.

One day, early in 2008, Stefan and I visited Berlin with Mr. Evil. Berlin and Brandenburg offered very attractive grant programs – money for nothing, essentially, with employees for free. There, we met an engaged and ambitious guy from the government. He and Mr. Evil outlined a complicated plan, with various subsidiaries being founded and transfers of knowledge and money being conducted among these various subsidiaries in different states and countries. It soon became clear that he was devising an elegant scheme to funnel grant money from Germany into Switzerland, though – into his own pockets. In short, it was fraud.

Mr. Evil wanted us to be the CEOs of all these different subsidiaries, saying "I'll be in the background so that I don't slow you down." That was nice of him! It's always good for your ego to be offered the CEO position. Not only does it signify power, but it also means that you'll be the one going to prison in the event of the fraud being discovered. Speaking of prison, the ambitious individual from the grant program was later imprisoned for fraudulent activities involving grant money being invested in an industrial complex in Brandenburg.

Later that day, at Tegel, the old airport in Berlin, Stefan and I looked at each other and said: "No. Not with us. We must get out of here. We have to get Mr. Evil out of NanoTemper!" Then we boarded the Air Berlin flight to Munich and started our next mission impossible: to oust Mr. Evil from our business.

All our assets were in the NTTAG that was registered in Baar, Switzerland, where Mr. Evil lived. He held the highest position in the company, as Swiss laws mandated that this role could only be occupied by someone residing in Switzerland. We couldn't do anything without his signature. The whole situation looked devastatingly bad for us! There was no straightforward way out, and we had no money left to pay world-class attorneys. We wondered if this might be the end of the NanoTemper story – before it had even begun.

This had all happened because we had succumbed to the temptation of big and easy money, having been blinded by his story about a shortcut to becoming very rich. In following this path, however, we nearly became tangled up in a fraud involving government grants and taxes. I had betrayed my own principles for money – and I was paying for it bitterly.

This stress, together with Mr. Evil playing us against each other, nearly destroyed my friendship with Stefan. I wish I had had our Code of Honor back then. In the end, only our sense of justice saved us from this huge mistake and got us back on the right path. We stopped working against each other, stopped working for Mr. Evil, and started to work toward our vision again, together. Staying true to yourself makes you unstoppable!

Was the Swiss disaster going to stop us? No! Stefan and I had such a strong belief in our idea that we kept fighting for it. Although we couldn't act without Mr. Evil in the Swiss NTTAG, we could still operate in Munich, so in May 2008 we founded the German NanoTemper Technologies GmbH there – the global company that you know today.

Our most valuable assets were our two patent applications. We used a borderline trick to transfer the patent applications from the Swiss NTTAG to the German NanoTemper GmbH. With some luck, we finally found some clever attorneys who helped us prevent Mr. Evil from acting, by removing him from his operational role. Fortunately, the attorneys didn't realize that we wouldn't have had the money to pay them if things had gone wrong.

Mr. Evil and the Swiss NTTAG remained in Switzerland, however, and our future would always be in danger with this Sword of Damocles hanging over our heads. Who would invest in us, given such a situation? Or buy products from us? We had to wipe the slate clean.

The NTTAG had to disappear – it had to be liquidated. As a liquidator, you are responsible for any outstanding liabilities. We faced a big unknown:

had Mr. Evil made large expenditures in the company's name that we were not aware of? If you don't take any risks, you risk everything. We took the risk, and we were lucky. There were no major outstanding debts. We were able to liquidate NTTAG and pave the way for our new future.

Fortune favors the brave. During the liquidation process, we received a very surprising phone call – an unknown voice with a strong Bavarian dialect introduced itself as a member of a Bavarian tax investigation team. They were hunting for Mr. Evil, who had already been involved in some sort of tax fraud. Since that call, we have not heard from Mr. Evil again. He has gone for good!

This Swiss disaster is why my advice to all founders is: don't give away your shares easily, especially not to someone you don't really know. It's nearly impossible to remove someone once they're in.

I learned to never stop believing. It was a very difficult time, with us and our project NanoTemper always being close to bankruptcy. During this period, thankfully, we had strong support from people like Sonja, from our university's patent office, and Christoph, from the university's spin-off and technology transfer department, who saved us more than once. They believed in us, empowered us, and helped us move on. A network of strong integral people is worth more than gold.

Trust is what saves you in the end: belief in your principles and mutual trust among your founders. It is this strong trust in one another that makes Stefan and I unstoppable together.

In every challenging situation we've faced – and there have been many – Stefan and I have reflected on our Swiss disaster: how we managed to overcome it together. This intense experience has since become a powerful source of strength for us.

FUNDING IN THE FINANCIAL CRISIS

Funding a biotech startup in Europe is a challenging endeavor. Even in favorable times, finding someone who is interested in investing in your business idea often requires luck. Now, imagine the situation during a financial crisis! We sought funding in 2008, right after Lehman Brothers had collapsed. The focus then was entirely on the survival of the banks themselves. Financing a risky startup? They all said "No thank you!"

The Swiss disaster was still raw when we pitched our idea at a VC and Business Angel brunch at the Spatenhaus at the Opera restaurant in Munich. It was held upstairs, on the first floor of a traditional Bavarian restaurant featuring a lot of wooden furniture, with a typical smell of beer, roast pork, and stale air.

50 businessmen wearing expensive yet old-fashioned suits were having brunch while we pitched our idea to them. It felt as though we were some kind of attraction – like actors who were there to entertain them. Despite our best efforts, most of them paid more attention to their food than to our business idea. Money was king and we were nothing: we felt disrespected. The feedback we received was: "Oh, you need less than 1 million in funding. Come to us again if you need 10 million. 1 million is not worth our work."

After further meetings with investors, it felt as though we were going to have to inflate our business concept in order to get funding. One group told us: "We only invest in software and IT – it offers a better and faster return on investment than biotechnology." Obviously, we were pitching our idea to the wrong audience. Unfortunately, though, all the audiences we presented to were similar to this one: Early Bird Ventures, Wellington Partners, MIG Capital, and others – we tried them all! Despite our best efforts, with our fancy pitch decks and polished talks, we couldn't convince any of them to invest in us.

VC and us... Looking back now, it was a clash of cultures from the very beginning. We needed other sources of funding.

Fortunately, however, there was Prof. Hermann, the holder of the biophysics chair, who supported us with 20,000 euros. He had founded the nanotech startup Nanotype some years earlier and knew how important every euro was for us. Additionally, we benefited from the EXIST seed funding for startups and the Bavarian FLÜGGE program.

FLÜGGE – what a name! It stands for Förderprogramm für einen leichteren Übergang in eine Gründer Existenz (Support Program for an Easier Transition to Being a Founder). This program funded two positions of 20 hours per week, plus we also received 5,000 euros per year for running costs. The best part? We gained access to the university's infrastructure, allowing us to utilize all the fancy high-tech equipment and various rooms for free. This was a game-changer for us. Even so, it was still nowhere near enough money for a biotech startup.

So, what do you do when you don't have money? You don't spend money. You keep costs low – very low.

You build fluorescence filter sets from waste. If you can't afford the complex measurement technology you need, you become creative and focus on the one simple thing making the greatest impact. You can't hire people, so we both worked double time: 60–80 hours per week became normal for us. Life/work balance? Our NanoTemper was our life!

Over this period, we learned a lot about financial discipline. Having no money available was a catalyst for us. We had to concentrate on one idea, one product. Ideas alone are worthless: the value is in their execution. Interesting? You'll read more about that in the following sections...

Winning business plan competitions as a business model

Still lacking sufficient income, we became creative and turned to business plan competitions as a source of funding. We had learned how to write business plans at Lars' seminar, then won an award at the Munich Business Plan Competition, so we aimed to secure money by winning more of these.

We learned a lot from this experience. First, we needed to understand how these competitions operated. Your goal is not to write a business plan for your own future business. No, you write the business plan to win the business plan competition. This is your one and only task.

Second, the timing is also crucial. If a biotech idea won the year before, there is a lower probability that your biotech idea will win again the following year. The competitions prefer to have winners from different areas, to maintain high engagement. Indeed, business plan competitions are run like businesses – they must attract sponsors and attendees to thrive.

After learning that it was never about the actual business plan itself, we once submitted the same plan to four different competitions. We won one, got a second prize in another, and received nothing at all in the other two competitions. What we soon realized is that whenever we presented in front of a jury, we secured either first, second, or third place. Authenticity, empathy, and a strong belief in our technology were key. Whenever we got the jury laughing, it went very well. My favorite answer to the question "What could go wrong with your technology?" was: "If it doesn't work, then we have failed – we have done something wrong. The technology itself is awesome."

We won the CyberOne Award in 2009, receiving a wonderful video as well as 10,000 euros, but I take the greatest pride in winning the Step Award – we tried five times before finally achieving that one. Never surrender! We were presented with the Step Award trophy at a Gala Dinner at the Messe Turm, a skyscraper in Frankfurt. In addition to the trophy, we received 100,000 euros – a crucial financial boost for us.

Given what I've just written, you might now be wondering whether a business plan is helpful. It's a valid question – and yes, it is! It goes beyond just winning competitions. Writing down your business idea in a structured manner, discussing it with your team, and obtaining external feedback constitute a significant early asset, even when you're bootstrapping your company. It's always wise to have a detailed plan for the next year and a less detailed one for the next three years. While revenue can often be difficult to predict, you can keep costs under control.

Winning business plan competitions also enhances your reputation. Business experts have reviewed and positively judged your work, which increases trust among third parties. Additionally, you receive helpful publicity and complimentary press releases, which are beneficial at the start of your journey.

Typically, a comprehensive infrastructure surrounds these business plan competitions, including advisors and experts on patents, trademarks, business plan writing, general administration, and more. Most importantly, you can connect with other founders. For us, the Munich Business Plan Competition was the first step in building a strong network, including the founders of companies like Coriolis and Chromotek.

BOOTSTRAPPING WITH A BUSINESS ANGEL

As we had previously had a positive experience with a grant, we continued to seek additional funding in this way, targeting the significant "KMU-innovative" award from the German Ministry of Science and Education (BMBF). If we were to win this one, it would finance us for nearly three years and ultimately enable us to develop a product.

Stefan and I focused entirely on this grant, doing nothing else. We conducted numerous experiments to provide supportive data and spent four weeks writing the grant application. Of course, it was no surprise that, despite our best efforts, we ended up submitting it at the last minute, with some panic being caused when we received an error message from the server.

Then we had to wait – and waiting is the most challenging task for entrepreneurs. Finally, we received a printed letter in the mail. We had a technical yes! The experts were convinced and the jury said go!

However, the financial team was not as supportive. They asked the following: "Please show us how you will counterfinance the grant." So back to the funding problem we returned. We needed money to start the grant – a lot of money, at least 300,000 euros. Where could we get that?

We at least had a good argument now: if you invest in NanoTemper, your money will be bolstered by this governmental grant.

We'd received the technical go message in June 2008, but by September, we still had no clue how to access the funds. And the deadline was approaching: no money, no grant, no NanoTemper, and almost no time left...

During this period, I learned to sleep even with this high pressure. Why? After the Swiss disaster, we had the experience as well as the belief that together we could manage anything. We would find the money, one way or another. We just had to keep trying hard, looking for it everywhere. And we had to trust in ourselves.

We'd been to many places and meetings to connect with venture capitalists and Business Angels – including Bavarian restaurants, as you've read about before. We'd pitched extensively, presenting our business plan and idea numerous times.

One of our last remaining hopes was the High Tech Gründer Fund (HTGF), which at the time had only recently been founded. Although this involved VC, it was ultimately a public–private partnership, with the Federal Ministry of Economics and Technology as a leading investor. The fund's main purpose is seed investment in deep-tech companies like NanoTemper. We were convinced that this kind of VC could work. We arranged a meeting to pitch our idea and were full of hope. We uploaded our PowerPoint slides, pressed "F5" for presenter mode, then action!

The reaction of the audience was a devastating surprise – the experts half-listened to us while typing messages on their BlackBerries. Those messages, it seemed, were more relevant to them than our idea. Needless to say, we didn't capture their interest and were unable to convince them. We simply couldn't present a 1 billion euro business idea, a moonshot. We were seen as too risky and too small – plus we didn't excel at pitching to them. Our last remaining hope seemed dead.

Then, one day, the money found us. At a place where we never expected it. It was during the open house day at LMU. Our professor asked whether we would showcase our research setup, saying that "The visitors would love to see what scientists do in biotechnology and nanotechnology." So we took our research setup to the large entrance hall of the university and presented our technology there. Our setup resembled a black shoebox but produced impressive high quantum yield camera movies of molecules moving around at a temperature gradient of a million degrees Celsius per meter. Science fiction in action!

We received a lot of attention. And then Volker stood in front of us: a prominent Munich real estate baron in his late 60s – and a self-made entrepreneur. He was very interested in science, particularly life sciences, as his youngest son had juvenile diabetes. He stopped in front of us. We explained the science to him, along with our business idea. He handed us his business card: "Let's meet – my assistant Barbara will organize it."

We'd found our Business Angel!

Despite the Swiss disaster, the challenging economic situation, and our lack of experience, Volker believed in us! He was willing to invest his own personal money – several hundred thousand euros. What a commitment! It felt amazing that he trusted us so deeply that he was happy to invest money that he had earned with his own hands. His investment saved us at the last minute. We signed the contract with him at the notary and sent it to the BMBF. The counterfinancing was complete. We secured the grant and leveraged Volker's investment with it. We didn't need any further investments. We had enough to grow NanoTemper and achieve profitability.

Volker, being a very experienced self-made entrepreneur, as well as a multi-millionaire, was an impressive person. We have learned a lot from him, especially in dealing with banks. He never disturbed us in our business, only asking us to keep him regularly informed. He was always there for us when we needed advice or a loan. I am also a Business Angel now, because of the great experience I had with him. Volker inspired me to be like him and to offer both money as well as experience to entrepreneurs. From him, I learned the importance of giving back.

NanoTemper was bootstrapped. At least, that's how we referred to it, since we only had support from one Business Angel. Many ask "Should I bootstrap? Should I seek VC funding?" There is no straightforward answer to this. Your primary task is to build and grow your startup. Most importantly, it's about finding a way to survive. With little money, you must pursue every available option and opportunity simultaneously, to increase your chances. After all, funding is just a tool to help you achieve your goals.

In NanoTemper's case, many experts advised us to pursue VC, which is a typical option for a deep-tech startup. Would we have taken VC funding at the beginning? Yes. But as you've read over the last few pages, we tried and we didn't get it, as we simply didn't meet their expectations. They considered us too risky, which I never fully understood. Isn't taking risks the very reason for the "venture" in venture capital?

We were in touch with a good VC fund for a long time. They initially told us "We first want to see that you sell a product." After we sold our first product to Crelux GmbH in 2010 (you'll read more about that soon), we approached them again. They responded "This was just luck, and you sold it to friends. Come back when you've sold 10 products." We were still too risky an investment for them. We then became so busy selling our products that we never returned for a third time.

As a sidenote, we won the German Prize for Innovation (Deutscher Innovationspreis) in early 2012, which was celebrated with a grand event at the Hotel Bayerischer Hof in Munich. When Bon Jovi, Robbie Williams, or other celebrities are in the city, they stay at this hotel. As you can imagine, it's a very cool location, and it was a lovely celebration with great publicity. After receiving this award, the same VC fund reached out to us once more, asking "Are you still interested in our investment?" Having been profitable for two years, they would only face a small risk by investing in us. However, we were no longer interested. We could double our revenue each year from our own profits alone. The money you earn from your products and customers is the best source of funding.

I really enjoy sharing our success story about bootstrapping and our Business Angel. Yes, the beginning was quite challenging. Keeping costs low – very low – is essential, and that's not enjoyable. You wouldn't want to see some of the places where I slept in order to save money. Nor the crazy car rides in the dark: from Berlin to Munich at 10:00 p.m., then from Munich to Basel at 6:00 a.m. There wasn't much sleep at all, in fact. There was no glamor. Nothing romantic. But we have been and still are independent. We didn't want to work to enrich a shareholder: we wanted to work for ourselves, simply because we wanted to – even if we were each working double time in the early days!

Bootstrapping, VC, bank loans, grants? The important thing is that you have options to choose from. That you have entrepreneurial freedom. That the decision is yours. It's your journey, and I can only share my experience with VC, while others share theirs. If VC enables you to execute your vision, then so be it.

My only advice is this: don't build your company solely to sell it. At least try to create a profitable and lasting business.

Stop developing and start selling

As you know, NanoTemper is a deep-tech company and a university spin-off. What is typical for all of us deep-tech startups is that we start with supercool and innovative technologies. Yeah, we'll rock it!

However, technologies are not products or solutions that you can easily sell. Customers don't buy the technologies themselves. Rather, they buy things that solve a problem for them, that benefit their careers, or that simply provide enjoyment.

Another problem that I alluded to earlier is that your technology offers you thousands of possibilities. Too many to pursue all of them. With biophysical measurement technology, for instance, you could target business-to-business markets like academic research, explore in vitro diagnostics, or provide various services. You could even venture into the consumer market, such as food testing or pregnancy tests.

So we soon had to decide which of the options we should choose. Here's the thing: if you don't risk anything, you risk everything. You have to pursue one option. In doing so, you have to risk one of the other options, which you've decided not to pursue, being a better one.

And this is good. You only have limited resources. If you spread them too thin, over too many projects, you will surely fail. If you concentrate everything on one project, you might fail, but you could also win. This is what you have to do – play to win.

Not surprisingly, we got it wrong during the first 18 months, trying many different approaches simultaneously. The result: no significant progress in any direction. This was until Mirko told us to "Just focus. Just build a device and try to sell it." Mirko was an advisor helping us with marketing and sales. This one time, we listened to him and followed his advice. This became our breakthrough. Given that you are holding this book in your hands, you already know that focusing on one device, on building one biophysical instrument, was what worked for us.

Gernot, our intern, built a research setup that was close enough to a prototype for us to be able to use for demos and for taking test measurements for customers. We were so proud of this that we even showcased our simple black box research setup at the huge Analytica

Tradeshow in Munich. One of our competitors from FluIT Biosystems laughed at us. We noted their much fancier design. They had VC funding and had built a very complex and sophisticated Fluorescence Correlation Spectroscopy measurement instrument. At first, it made us feel bad – we had just done our best with what we had. But their repeated disrespect further motivated us to focus on our one product, to make its technology and design even better.

As a funny sidenote, NanoTemper went on to become a profitable company. FluIT Bioysystems later went bankrupt – the one who had laughed at us at the trade show subsequently applied for an R&D position with us, but he wasn't a fit for our culture.

Why has NanoTemper been so successful? The one thing that we did differently from other startups is that we invested in sales very early on – as the purpose of a private company is to generate revenue and achieve profitability. So, if you were to ask me "Who should be my first hire – a developer or a salesperson?" My answer will always be "The salesperson." You can only earn money when you are selling.

Here's the good news: you, the founder(s), are the best salesperson(s). Why? Because you live your business. You fully understand it. Your customers will feel this and trust you. Trust is what triggers purchase decisions. Go out. Leave the lab. Go where your customers are. Stop developing and start selling! It won't be easy, though – you'll fail a lot, but you'll also learn a lot from these failures.

Once we organized a demo at the MPI in Göttingen. A big shot invited us. If this works and he buys, we'll have it, we thought. Stefan and I packed our demonstrator into the white high-speed Intercity Express train to Göttingen.

It was a black box, which was heavy like a crate of beer. We arrived in Göttingen on time – thank you, Deutsche Bahn! – and then took the bus to the MPI at Faßberg, which is on a hill. Suddenly, the bus stopped: it was damaged. Jesus! The things that can go wrong! We got out of the bus and together carried the heavy demonstrator for the last kilometer to the MPI. The demonstrator survived. We measured the samples and got results that looked good to us. He didn't buy. We had failed again. But our failure in this instance was that we didn't ask in advance what would trigger a purchase decision for him.

Despite all the obstacles and risks that you'll face, focus on selling what you already have, whether it's a concept paper, a mock-up, or a research setup. You'll learn from the sales conversation how your product should look. Only by asking a customer to buy your product and spend money on you will you receive the concrete feedback necessary to finalize your product. Always remember, you don't develop the product for yourself, you develop it for your customers, so that they'll buy it.

Money is a very good source of information. People will only give you their money if they stand to benefit from your product. They will only purchase your innovation when it has a positive impact on them. This is essential knowledge for your product development. Only create what people want or need and what they are willing to pay for. Follow the money!

THE BREAKTHROUGH – FIRST SALES

It was 23 December 2009, and I was in our lab in the cellar of LMU. I was taking measurements for the Munich biotech company Crelux GmbH, working intensely on our research setup. Ismail and Michael, the Chief Science Officer and CEO (and also founders) of Crelux GmbH, had told us: "If you can get these small molecule–kinase interactions working, we'll purchase your Monolith NT.015 instrument."

We had a clear goal. We had agreed on what would trigger their buying decision. I can't remember ever working with such concentration and dedication. Not only did I want it to work, so that Crelux GmbH would buy, but I also wanted to finish, so that I could drive to see my family for Christmas.

Late in the evening, I gathered all the data, wrote the report, and sent both the data and the report to Crelux. I then left the lab and drove to my family, located 270 km north of Munich.

On 9 January 2010, Ismail from Crelux responded: "Your data looks good; we'll buy your Monolith." We received a pre-payment of 10,000 euros from them. We purchased the parts, built our first prototype, the Monolith NT.015, and painted it among the trash cans in the university cellar. It wasn't the prettiest creation, but it worked.

Selling your first instrument is like having your first kiss: you'll never forget it. Although it's a long time ago, I can still remember every detail from that day, 23 December 2009, including having *Watchmen* running on the streaming platform kino.to. Everything! That's a memory for eternity.

Here's our proven algorithm for reaching profitability:

START
(
Sell the first prototype before it is built -> Get prepayment -> Build instrument, paint it black, deliver and support it -> Keep every promise made.
From the profit of the first sale:
Build the next instrument -> Demo -> Convince -> Deliver -> Support.
)
REPEAT

We repeated this many times in 2010. By the end of the year, we had sold 29 prototypes. We've been profitable ever since.

This was all possible because of our sales to Crelux GmbH, which enabled us to find our niche – the measurement of small molecules, even molecular fragments. These have a very low mass. Which was a good thing for us: all the other biophysical measurement methods on the market were mass-dependent. They struggled to measure such small and light molecules.

Our method was based on a different principle, however – it was independent of mass and size. Therefore, small molecules that are nearly impossible for others to measure were easy for us. This is what you can call a USP (unique selling proposition). Fortunately for us, there was considerable hype about fragment-based drug discovery around 2010, and we just capitalized on it.

You may wonder: how was it possible for us to sell 29 instrument prototypes in less than a year?

We focused nearly everything we had on selling and building the Monolith NT.015 prototypes. To do so, we hired Moran, an Israeli biologist with outstanding sales skills. Stefan, Moran, and I handled the sales. Gernot and Hüseyin constructed the devices and improved them on the fly in response to customer feedback. As a result, the first 29 instruments were all different, each one being an improvement on the previous prototype. During this time, we didn't engage in anything that you could call R&D. There was truly a full focus on the business and securing funds.

The 29 Monolith NT.015 prototypes we sold were not only a financial success, but also provided a lot of helpful user feedback for the development of our final production instrument, the Monolith NT.115. I'm still very proud that the biotechnology company Roche Kulmbach GmbH, from my hometown of Kulmbach (with just 26,000 residents), bought one of our first production Monolith devices.

Do you have a technology and are you currently developing your first product? Are you asking yourself: "When will it be ready and when should I start selling it?" The answer is now, immediately, today!

Your first product is ready for sale whenever you decide to sell it.

When your product doesn't kill, burn down a building, or otherwise harm people, you can only learn by exposing it to your customers.

SUMMARY

MY PERSONAL SHIFT MOMENT

During the period from 2007 to 2010, our startup nearly died before it had even begun, because we found ourselves trapped in a fraudulent scheme in Switzerland. Scammed by someone we trusted, we lost our money and almost lost each other.

From this near-collapse in Switzerland to selling our first product, I learned that vision alone doesn't build a company: resilience, focus, and early sales do.

- We had to learn this the hard way: never give away your shares easily, especially not for promises — even if family is involved, it is nearly impossible to get a bad person out again.

- We were rejected by every major German VC firm during the 2008 financial crisis and had to scrape together funding from grants and business plan contests, while maintaining our personal belief.

- I discovered that starting to sell matters more than continuing to develop: our survival depended on getting customers, not building the perfect product.

- Our first sale didn't come from a fancy pitch — it came from obsession, grit, and a willingness to ask real buying questions. That changed everything.

NanoTemper Technologies GmbH was born out of chaos. Not out of confidence or capital, but out of a refusal to quit – and out of a relentless focus on turning invention into revenue.

In 2010, our team grew from two to three members, and our revenue increased from zero to 1 million euros. We had already become profitable.

HOW THIS CHAPTER LIVES THE CODE OF HONOR

I build trust – or I build nothing

When we gave shares to someone we didn't truly know, we paid the price. Only my mutual trust with Stefan and the support of brave believers like Volker, our Business Angel, and Sonja, who fought for our patent rights at the university, saved us. Trust isn't a value – it's your shield.

I put people first – always

I nearly lost my co-founder and my best friend. But we rebuilt our partnership and protected each other. From working side by side for 80 hours a week to learning to lead our team in the lab, we realized the hard way that people are everything.

I scale smart and fast

In the beginning, we tried too many things at once and got nowhere. Then a mentor said "Just build a device and try to sell it." We listened, focusing on one product and one market and rejecting the other thousand ideas we had. That shift from scattered effort to focused action was our turning point: scaling isn't about doing more, it's about doing the right thing.

I build a profitable business that lasts

We didn't raise millions. We didn't inflate our numbers. We just sold what we had, made it better with every sale, and turned customer revenue into growth. Bootstrapping wasn't a strategy – it was survival. To only spend what we earned enabled us to remain independent.

I execute my vision
Even when others doubted or ignored us, we pushed forward. We sold our first prototype before it was built, turned a deposit into a product, and reinvested the profits again and again. We didn't discuss risks – we took them.

NOW OVER TO YOU

You don't need millions to start. You don't need perfect products or even a full team.

What you need is the courage to sell what you've got – and the discipline to build only what people are willing to pay for. Money is just a tool. Your mission, your people, and your customers: they constitute your engine.

CHALLENGE FOR YOU

What's the one product or service you can start selling right now, even if it's not finished?

Go out, show it, and ask "Would you buy this today?"

3: FROM FOUNDER TO ENTREPRENEUR – LEARNING LEADERSHIP THE HARD WAY

Starting a company is one thing, but leading it is another. I made every leadership mistake possible: pushing people too hard, trusting the wrong ones, and learning the painful truth that trust is much easier to lose than to regain.

Along the way, I realized that NanoTemper was more than just a business – it was a responsibility. A failed acquisition, an exit offer of 60 million dollars (which we rejected), and a growing team forced me to rethink everything.

LETTING GO TO GROW

"Managers grow by taking on responsibilities. Founders grow by delegating them over." Götz Werner, the founder of DM Drogeriemarkt, said this in

2014, when we received the German Founders Award at the ZDF television studio in Berlin. It has stuck with me.

In the early days, it was just Stefan and me. We both had the same vision, the same mission, and the same goal. We did everything together, at the same time – fast and in sync. Why change that? Because doing everything yourself doesn't scale. You can only grow if you delegate your responsibilities.

Delegating always feels strange and uncomfortable at first. Someone else may approach things differently, even if it leads to the same outcome. As a leader, you have to let go, stay out of the way, and trust your team. Otherwise, you risk demotivating the very people you need the most. Yes, it can be quicker to complete a task yourself than explain it to someone else – once. But, with a growing team, this logic breaks down. You must build for scale.

The best-case scenario is that you hire people who are better than you. That sounds obvious, but it's rarely done. Watching someone else excel at tasks you once completed yourself can bruise your ego. I still wrestle with that. Winning the internal battle is crucial...

Thankfully, I've won it often enough. Feedback from customers and partners shows that we have outstanding people at NanoTemper. Over time, I've delegated more and more to these promising talents. That's how growth happens: your key people step up and take over.

THE NINE LIVING HEARTS OF NANOTEMPER

People will come and go in any organization. Even a small company will see hundreds of arrivals and departures over a couple of decades. Each person is important and will shape the company in one way or another.

New people bring fresh energy and different perspectives. Leavers create space for renewal. Change is good: it opens our minds to education and constant learning.

With all this change, though, what remains constant? A handful of people who grow with your company, who understand how it works at its core, and who are willing to adapt and evolve alongside it. At NanoTemper, we have nine of these rare individuals. They embody our culture. When someone asks me "What is NanoTemper?" I picture them talking to one of these nine people.

You've already heard about Gernot, our Head of Production, who's been with us since 2009. The other eight joined between 2010 and 2015. When things get tough, they're the ones who always step up and rise to the occasion. I trust them completely. I am convinced that every successful company includes such hearts – people who joined the company at the very beginning and have grown with it for more than a decade. You will find them at Google, Microsoft, SAP, and Genentech, too.

These people are your diamonds. But you should know that despite being resistant to pressure, even diamonds burn. It is your duty as an entrepreneur to take care of them. My door, ears, and eyes are always open to them, no matter what. Don't waste time on the troublemakers in your team: invest in your core. They'll carry your vision forward alongside you.

LESSONS FROM THE EARLY TEAM

Of our first 10 employees, Gernot is the only one who is still with us. Starting as an intern, he developed and built the initial Monolith prototypes and now leads global production. As for the others who departed, it was mostly my fault – I was a terrible boss in those days.

Take Hüseyin, for instance, a shy but kind electronics engineer who joined us straight from university, after completing his Master's thesis, in August 2009, and stayed with us until September 2010. It is so difficult to find good engineers and I treated him poorly. I shouted at him, I didn't trust him, and I belittled him in front of others. He was better than me – and I resented it. He understood electronics much better than me and often had different opinions. Instead of learning from him, I let my frustration show. It's no wonder that he left. Being a great guy, he completed the Monolith NT.115 before going – the device that allowed us to break into the US market.

My next failure was Iman, a foreign student who interned with us. Because she had funded her own position, I wrongly assumed that she wasn't competent and treated her accordingly. I thought she would never accomplish anything and would not go far in her career. She later became Miss New York City and founded her own AI company. She's famous now and I couldn't have been more wrong about her.

Others joined and left too – Svenja, Sabine, Chris, and Max. We worked in dark rooms, under huge pressure and for little appreciation. It's no wonder they moved on. The lesson? People don't just leave bad jobs – they vote with their feet.

Looking back, I was a bad boss. But I had never had a great boss myself. I went straight from being a PhD student to being a CEO, learning by doing. That might sound like a fast track, but for my team, it was often a painful experience. I didn't put people first – and I let them down.

HOW TO HIRE FOR GROWTH

Reflecting on these early mistakes, I realized that becoming a better leader meant learning how to hire with vision, not with desperation. Growth brings complexity, and the people you bring in can shape your company more than anything else. You also have to hire the right people at the right time. The art lies in identifying talent, attitude, and growth potential during the interview process.

Over the years, I've reviewed more than 20,000 CVs and interviewed more than 1,700 candidates. Here are a few of the things that I've learned:

1. Everyone enjoys hiring. But you don't solve problems by simply bringing in more people. Your fixed costs will skyrocket and finally kill you.

2. Trust your gut feeling. Of all the people I've hired, those I had doubts about after the interview rarely stayed longer than 12 months.

3. If, after 10 minutes, you think "I'd be stupid not to hire this person," that's a positive signal to hire this person immediately.

4. If you need someone urgently, to fill a critical role, don't compromise and hire someone just because you're in a hurry. This will slow you down – twice. First, you'll waste time by hiring the wrong person, who you'll later have to let go. And second, you'll need to go through the entire hiring and onboarding process for a second time.

5. Don't be afraid of making mistakes. Utilize probation periods – they're a useful tool for both sides. Ending things early is also fair to your employee, because it saves both of you time.

6. The onboarding process begins with the initial job interview. If you handle it well, you'll gain a fan of your company. If you handle it poorly, you may lose an employee before the journey has truly begun.

I've made mistakes in relation to all of these points, especially the fourth one (which I'll further explore in a following story): urgency is the enemy of good reflection. The more you're in a hurry, the more mistakes you'll make. Take your time over all people-related issues, because it's time that is well invested. Stay in control, and don't let an urgent process control you.

Most importantly, hire people for what they can do in the future, not just for what they've done in the past. I learned this the hard way when we started building our executive team. We hired impressive people who had managed thousands of employees at major corporations. On paper, they were exactly who we needed to scale. But many couldn't adapt to the different reality of a founder-led business trying to grow from 200 to 1,000 people.

Managing complexity at scale is a different skill than helping a company grow toward that complexity. I was too impressed by where they had come from and didn't look closely enough at whether they could grow with us. Since then, I've learned to prioritize mindset, adaptability, and a willingness to learn over a polished track record.

The Waldemar lesson

After Hüseyin left, we were in trouble. He was our only software developer, and the only person who fully understood the software running our instruments. As we were a startup, structured documentation and software architecture weren't priorities – speed was. Without Hüseyin, we couldn't fix bugs, improve usability, or push new features. And if customers were to start complaining, our brand reputation would be at risk. We had to find someone fast.

This urgency meant that we overlooked the importance of a long-term fit. It showed me what can happen when you ignore your gut, rush to fill a seat, and mistake experience for adaptability.

That's when we found Waldemar – a veteran physicist-turned-programmer who had been coding since the days of punched cards. He stabilized our software, made it more robust, and reduced system crashes. Customers noticed the improvement. We were relieved.

But something felt off. He resisted collaboration. One day, I brought him a bug report from a customer. "That's not a bug," he snapped: "First, we need to define whether it's user error or an actual software issue."

What followed was not a pragmatic discussion about fixing the problem, but a philosophical debate regarding the definition of a bug. Our strategy was built on superior ease of use. Yet here we were with a developer who saw customers as adversaries instead of partners. And then he started avoiding us! His work hours shifted later and later. The once-collaborative atmosphere in our basement office turned into one of silence and isolation.

But then we hired Axel, the best product developer I've ever met. Axel is one of the few people who can fully grasp what a "product" is, both technically and commercially. He had only been with us for a week when he pulled me aside and said "If Waldemar stays, I leave." This was a bold statement from a very new employee.

Axel explained that Waldemar was blocking him, hiding code, and refusing to share knowledge. I started digging deeper and found that Waldemar had built the software in a way that made him irreplaceable. He had locked us into dependence on him.

I had two choices:

1. keep Waldemar, knowing he was creating a long-term liability; or
2. rip off the Band-Aid and take control of the future.

That night, I didn't sleep. My thoughts went back and forth: the longer Waldemar stayed, the more damage he could do, and the more difficult he would be to replace.

The next day, when he arrived late, as usual, I met him at the door: "Waldemar, I have to terminate your contract. Please take your belongings and go."

Months later, we met again – this time in court. We had proposed a severance package, which Waldemar didn't accept. So the court had to decide what to do about it. Despite already having another job, Waldemar demanded to be reinstated.

In the court, the judge called our severance package a fair one and proposed a settlement. At this point, Waldemar told the judge that he (not the judge) should be the one to decide whether the settlement was fair. It was a public hearing and the room murmured: this was unbelievable to us and to everyone in the room! The judge was also speechless, at first, before ruling for the settlement agreement. Our experienced attorney told us that he had never been through anything like this. End of story.

The whole ordeal reinforced what I'd learned: if someone is working against the company, act quickly and end the employment relationship immediately. Waiting will only make things worse. The other person's power will strengthen over time. No one, not even your best expert, should hold your company hostage. Over 19 years, I've learned that you'll always find someone new. It won't get better or worse – it just becomes different.

Letting Waldemar go also taught me a vital lesson: firing someone is never easy. Nor should it be. If you feel bad, that's good – it means you care. But parting ways is sometimes necessary to protect the company and its culture. You must accept that not everyone you hire will stay. This isn't a family or a friendship – it's a business. The best companies know how to onboard and offboard well.

If someone is toxic, act immediately, even if they're talented. Their presence will damage your culture and drive your best people away. You won't always get direct complaints, so stay alert. Ask team leaders for honest feedback. Create space for whistleblowers. Once you remove the toxic element, people will often tell you how relieved they are. Every time, I think "Why didn't you say something sooner?"

I hate letting people go, but it's often led to NanoTemper's biggest growth leaps. I do it thoughtfully: I try to be honest, prepared, and respectful. Sometimes I help them find new roles. But if they were toxic with us, I won't pass the problem to someone else.

MY FIRST LAYOFF

Not every dismissal is about toxicity, however. Some are about trust and heartbreak. One of the hardest moments of my career accompanied my first layoff.

Tears and a shot of hard liquor in a bar. A crying single mom. And me feeling absolutely awful. There was no easy solution – I'd been forced to make the decision to protect NanoTemper.

We had developed a technology that could measure things in ways that hadn't been possible before. That means that people have to trust your results, especially when there's no way to cross-check them. My first layoff was about lost trust.

With extensive experience, a sharp mind, a wonderful personality, and a short modern hairstyle, she started as a scientist, with the job of conducting demo measurements using customer samples. These measurements prove that our products work. And we also have to earn the trust of our customers throughout the process.

She did an excellent job, always getting the expected results. She never failed. But this made me suspicious: new technology typically has a high failure rate, so something didn't feel right.

I raised it with her once. She presented me with strong arguments, which I believed, but the feeling didn't go away.

So I did something I'm not proud of: I tested her. I provided her with a reaction tube filled with nothing but water – you must understand that all our samples appear like pure water, due to the extremely low concentrations. I told her that it contained an antibody and that the customer expected strong binding to one of seven antigens. It looked like every other sample.

And sure enough, she reported strong binding. But there was no antibody. Fraud! She had faked the result!

I freaked out. We have only sold on trust. We were founded on trust. If we were found to be faking the demo data for our customers, that would kill NanoTemper forever.

She explained that she felt intense pressure to deliver, that she was afraid we'd fail as a company, and that she needed the salary to support her child. While I understood what she said, I still couldn't excuse it. As much as I wanted to help her as a person, as an Honorable Entrepreneur, I simply couldn't. Our company was built on trust – and if we lost that, we'd lose everything.

I gave her her notice, before we cried in each other's arms. I bought her a German Jägermeister. Then she was gone.

I still think about that day. It taught me that sometimes, even when you understand someone's reasons, you still have to act. You can recover lost money. But trust? Once it's gone, it's gone.

As an entrepreneur, that's your currency. Protect it fiercely. And never forget that your people are the ones who carry it forward – or let it fall.

Trust builds the foundation. But to grow, you also need space to expand.

MOVING ON UP

In 2011, we were still in the cellar of LMU – more specifically, in the former materials store for the mechanic's workshop. There were two small barred windows. There was light sometimes, but it wasn't pleasant. It worked at the very beginning. As things moved on, though, it was no longer an environment for attracting people or encouraging creativity and inspiration. Long story short, we had to get out of there!

Volker, our Business Angel, was our go-to person. As a real estate business owner, he helped us find our first proper home for NanoTemper – the "Werkstadt Sendling."

We moved to the fourth floor of a refurbished 1960s industrial building. We could see the German Alps from there. We rented 600 square meters for 10 years – a huge empty space, where we initially set up an espresso machine and a foosball table. Renting this large space was a significant commitment and thus a considerable risk for us.

The refurbished industrial building had once been a cigarette factory. As you probably know, smoking is the highest risk factor for developing cancer – for men, in particular, it poses a greater risk than all other risk factors combined. And now we were developing and producing tools for cancer research there. What an irony!

Scientists recently utilized our instruments to target the beating heart of cancer: the so-called "KRAS" molecule – in many cancers, especially lung cancers, the KRAS molecule gets mutated, causing cells to grow out of control. The incidence of KRAS mutations is between 25% and 35% in smokers but only 5% in nonsmokers.

Having a nice home for NanoTemper in Munich, close to the river Isar, enabled us to grow and to persuade more and more great people to join us on our journey. Indeed, it worked so well that we expanded to 3,500 square meters in that same building. It was our home until March 2024, when it finally became too small. In April 2024, we moved into a new building 300 meters south, where we rented 7,000 square meters – plenty of space for our further growth.

A company's premises reflect its corporate culture. Our new space has many open and bright rooms, and most of the walls are made of glass. It's a great new home for us that feels very much like the right next step.

BECOMING PROFITABLE

Our new space gave us room to grow, but physical space alone doesn't build a company. To sustain that growth, we had to get serious about profitability – ASAP! That started with learning how to price. But therein lies a dilemma for many founders and entrepreneurs. At what price should I sell my product for? There are many books on this topic. The first reaction of most technology-driven founders is to consider the issue from the perspective of production costs and to opt for a low list price. This approach is WRONG!

There are two reasons why:

1. your production costs do not determine your sales price – the value you generate for your customers determines how much they are willing to pay; and
2. do not settle for cheap – aim for a premium price. Have you invented the best and most innovative new product on the market? Why should it be priced lower than other products? Being better means you can justify a higher price.

Your goal must be to become profitable as fast as possible. Here is the formula for it:

Profit = Revenue – Costs.

Obviously, your costs have to be lower than your revenue. Obviously, your production costs must be lower than your sales price.

Revenue can be expressed as the number of products sold multiplied by the sales price of each product: revenue = number of products * sales price per product. A higher sales price means you have to sell fewer products to achieve the same revenue. Selling a large number of products can be challenging at the beginning – consider the logistics and the complex supply chain involved. It will also take several years to learn how to produce your innovative products at high volume while maintaining good quality.

Given this, focus on low volume, high prices, and good quality at the beginning. Good quality will make your customers happy, which in turn will make you happy. Poor quality will quickly damage your reputation through word of mouth. A high sales price will enhance your profitability. Being profitable will then allow you to invest in your supply chain and production, enabling you to increase your volume without sacrificing quality.

Scale smart. Achieve rapid growth through small yet steady steps in a consistent direction. This approach will lead you to profitability more quickly than making large leaps with uncertain outcomes and high costs.

When we sold our first prototype – the Monolith NT.015 – for 20,000 euros, we quickly realized that that price was too cheap for us to be able to survive. We then improved the prototype with temperature control, transforming it into the NT.015T, which we sold for 35,000 euros. This was sufficient for survival but still not enough to grow our company.

We subsequently developed a production device that looked completely different and offered a much better user experience. With this aesthetically pleasing and otherwise improved product, the Monolith NT.115, we achieved a sales price of 90,000 euros. This price was a good one – it made us profitable and allowed us to grow from our profits.

Becoming profitable gave us confidence. But we knew it wasn't enough. If we wanted to build a truly global company, we had to take bold steps: greater ambition, a bigger market, and a strategy that could scale beyond Germany.

THINK BIG – GO GLOBAL

If you are a deep-tech company and you have a big vision, you want to scale, and you want to do it fast and smart, what do you do?

You must conquer the US. The US is the largest single market in our world, especially for technology. Here, you will find many first movers and early adopters, as well as many customers eager to invest in new products.

Many European founders I speak with are afraid to enter the US market. They hesitate for years. I understand their fear of this vast and dynamic market. However, fear is not a valid reason to avoid entering it. Execute your vision: think big, go global – head to the US!

Entering a foreign market is always challenging, simply because it isn't your home market. In your home market, you know all the rules and have an established network. But a foreign market is *terra incognita*: you must explore it, and it often takes between three and five years until you are truly immersed in it.

No matter how big your fear of entering your largest foreign market, just do it. The market won't wait for you. If you don't seize the opportunity, your competition will.

Yes, we'd sold our first 29 prototypes in Europe. But then we immediately moved beyond our home market. The first production Monolith NT.115 instrument? That went to the US – to the Children's Hospital in Cincinnati.

As was usual for us, we sold it before we'd actually built it. Stefan and Moran took a flight to the US, and we started to build the device. Gernot, Hüseyin, and I built it together with Hans-Jörg, in his garage. Hans-Jörg was a hands-on freelance engineer, and together with the industrial design company Oxxid GmbH, we turned the protype into a production device. It has a cool design, which won a Red Dot Award, and it was much more user-friendly, with an automated door! It was ready for the US. In theory...

What followed was a bit crazy. It was like the Wild Wild West. We had to ship the device by Monday. We started building it on Friday. No one slept. We fixed bugs on the fly. Hüseyin was still writing the code. When it shipped, it was literally held together with duct tape. But it ran. And it arrived on time...

Stefan and Moran picked it up from the airport. They unpacked it, checked it, recalibrated it, and yes – it was able to measure. We were ready for an unforgettable and impactful four-week roadshow in the US with our first Monolith instrument.

During this road trip, Stefan and Moran faced a number of challenges, such as the new automatic door not opening because the instrument was still cold from the chilly night it had spent in the parked car. They then had to find a way of manually pushing up the door without the customer realizing. Sometimes a talent for acting can be very helpful...

At the National Institutes of Health, our host Jim introduced us by quoting Arthur C. Clarke: "Any sufficiently advanced technology is indistinguishable from magic." That's when we knew we were in the right place at the right time.

Yes, we were afraid to enter the US. But you never regret the risks you take. Only the ones you don't.

Moran had completed his PhD at the Children's Hospital, where his professor, Yi, became one of our earliest champions. He trusted Moran – and, by extension, he trusted us. Not only did he purchase a Monolith, but he also let us use his lab as a demo space.

That local connection made all the difference. American customers want to see that their peers trust you. Saying that you only have European customers will not convince a US-based customer. You need to get closer: "Ah, you have a Monolith at Professor Yi's lab at the Children's Hospital? I've heard one of his talks. It's a good institute." This general observation applies to other countries across the world. Business is local.

When most companies set up a US subsidiary, they head straight for Delaware, to save on taxes. But we didn't care about taxes – we cared about people. We built NanoTemper Inc. in the Bay area of California, because that's where Ana was. Ana wasn't just our first US hire, she ended up shaping our US business for more than a decade.

I first connected with Ana Lazic in December 2011, when she applied for a job that we'd posted on LinkedIn. Stefan invited her for a Skype interview on 19 December, which they scheduled for 21 December. The interview must have gone well, because just a few hours later, Stefan sent her an email inviting her to come to Munich.

We met in person on 5 January 2012. That evening, we went to dinner, and the following day, we negotiated her contract. Back then, we moved fast – really fast. I remember handing her a huge laptop computer and saying "The only problem is it has a German keyboard." She had to buy the biggest tote bag she could find to take it home in.

By 12 January, we had officially opened NanoTemper Inc. in the US. Sebastian, an attorney who specialized in transatlantic business relations, filed the paperwork with the Secretary of State, while ACG, our accounting and tax firm, handled the payroll and administrative setup.

Ana officially joined us on 1 February, and we signed her employment contract in person at the Biophysics Conference in San Diego on 24 February. What I didn't know at the time was that just a few days earlier, on

18 February, her father had passed away. She had flown to Serbia that day, then returned shortly afterward, still making it to the conference on time.

She started working immediately – before the company was fully operational in the US and before she even had an official contract. That's how we worked back then! Ana once wrote to me: "That's trust. That has impressed me strongly."

Every new business starts small and takes years to establish a local presence. We built the US company on trust and with a people-first approach. As of 2025, we have 47 people there. We later established ourselves in China, too, with Zhuo, and as of 2025, we have 21 people there. Zhuo has shaped and scaled our business in China for a decade.

The lesson: focus on local people to build your business first. Seek the city with the best opportunities and the most supportive community, not the one with the lowest taxes.

If your business doesn't flourish, you won't have the luxury of having to worry about taxes, so don't expend your energy on tax-saving strategies. If your local business becomes highly profitable, that will be due to the trust of your local customers. Therefore, it's only fair that you should pay the local taxes: they enable the government to maintain the infrastructure that serves your community – for me, this is a way of repaying the trust I have received.

SAW – OUR FIRST (AND ONLY) ACQUISITION

Here's a press release from 21 October 2014: "NanoTemper acquires SAW Instruments GmbH in Bonn." This has been our first (and only) acquisition to date. SAW Instruments was a competitor, and the biosensor space in Germany is small – we all knew one another.

In August 2014, Sabine, their CEO, called me: "My company is in trouble – we're not going to make it. Can we talk?" We visited them in Bonn. They were using a smartphone-frequency-filter-based technology called "Love waves" or "surface acoustic waves (SAW)," which had the potential to measure drug binding kinetics in living cells. Back then, we couldn't measure kinetics, so we were interested. But time was tight – they were running out of money and close to bankruptcy.

We initiated a red flag due diligence procedure with the law firm Pinsent Masons. We only had time for a coarse-grained overview, focusing on the biggest risks. In addition, we acquired one of SAW's instruments, to enhance their liquidity and examine their technology more closely. This gained us some weeks. We needed to make a quick decision, however, so we acted swiftly. We made them an offer – very low, as we understood the shareholders wanted to prevent insolvency. We quickly received the support of nearly all the shareholders, pleased that their ideas and technologies would endure. The shareholder with the smallest percentage of shares took the longest to agree to our offer, as he had a strong emotional connection. Within eight weeks, though, we completed the acquisition of our close competitor.

An interesting fact: one of the larger shareholders of SAW Instruments GmbH was the German HTGF, the VC fund that had rejected us in 2007 and 2008.

We were proud of our first acquisition. We invited the SAW team to our headquarters in Munich for a party. I can tell you, folks from Bonn sure know how to party! For 10 years afterward, there was one story that every new employee heard – involving a pink pattern on a white wall in our office and my dancing mishap with a bottle of red wine from the Rheinland!

The acquisition was cheap and initially felt like a win. But the integration? Well, that wasn't so good...

We made a few wrong assumptions:

- That the best and most passionate employees would stay until the end – like a captain who leaves the sinking ship last of all.
- That it's easy to manage eight people in Bonn while leading 58 in Munich, as traveling within Germany is easy-peasy.
- That you can handle foreign-acquired technology like your own invented technology.
- That the acquisition is the costly part.

Cultural clashes followed, with distractions from our key business areas, overestimation of the technological potential, and overestimation of our management skills.

There were also petty arguments between teams about how to pronounce SAW correctly: "Don't call it saw technology (like 'sawing') – you have to call it S-A-W technology! Single letters, please" and "Our technology is better than yours." These disputes and more consumed a lot of energy.

We soon realized that it made no sense to rebuild the shrinking SAW team in Bonn. Therefore, we relocated the SAW Instruments company to Munich.

The potential of SAW technology to measure the binding kinetics of ligands to living cells was something that we would never be able to reproduce. When the supplier of the SAW chips was acquired and we had to decide whether to invest millions in a new SAW chip design, to switch suppliers, we decided to stop.

The integration was halted, and we ceased our investment in this technology. Only in December 2022 was SAW Instruments GmbH removed from the commercial register.

It took eight weeks to acquire SAW and eight years to exit. Was this a mistake? Yes. But we had taken an educated risk. And we had failed. That's how it works: you try, you fail, and you learn along the way. Of course, we felt bad. It felt as though we had lost an important game. And I hate losing!

Looking back, though, I can see the whole thing in a better light, because I now know things I could not have known then. Stopping SAW freed up resources – resources that we subsequently invested in developing our Prometheus instrument, which launched in 2015, is now our best seller, and has become a gold standard in our industry.

We also learned that we should aim to acquire companies at an earlier and healthier stage.

Will we try again? Absolutely: I'm always on the lookout for new ideas, interesting technologies, and companies, especially when they can help us to scale faster and smarter.

POKERFACE – 60 MILLION DOLLARS ON THE TABLE

After navigating our first acquisition, I had thought that we were finally starting to find our footing. Then, not long after, there came a very different kind of offer – one that tested my values, not my spreadsheets.

One day, Tom and Jerry from California showed up at our office in the old cigarette factory. They were scouting companies for "Proteins Easy Inc." Stefan was away visiting customers, so I was alone with them.

They were good: they had more experience than I did and they were smooth and confident Americans, speaking their native tongue and playing the game at a higher level than me. I felt outmatched. They had a strategy for the meeting – I didn't. They applied pressure and also wanted to impress me.

Tom placed 60 million dollars on the table – metaphorically, of course. At the time, our revenue was 7 million euros, and we had 35 employees. It was massive multipler.

But I didn't flinch. I maintained my poker face. Stefan and I had agreed that we wouldn't sell, no matter the price. This was why he hadn't rescheduled his customer meeting.

Regardless of our agreement, I was still very surprised that having this amount of money on the table didn't elicit a reaction from me. It was an unbelievably large sum for someone who had received government support (Bafög) for my studies, because my parents couldn't support me financially.

Tom and Jerry simply couldn't believe my lack of reaction. For the first time, I saw some emotion on their faces. I mean, 60 million dollars for a biotech company employing 35 people with 7 million euros in revenue – that's a good price, isn't it?

Tom was very straightforward. He showed me his portfolio – acquisitions that had thrived in the US but flopped in Europe. I pointed that out. He didn't like it. His argument that we could grow more strongly under his umbrella didn't resonate with me either.

Then he closed his laptop. Jerry later told me that "If Tom closes his laptop like that, it means you really pissed him off."

We remained polite and the friendly talk continued for the next 10 minutes or so. But from that day onward, Tom and I were business rivals. I greatly appreciate his success – we can have brief and pleasant conversations. Overall, I view it like sport: good competition keeps you moving.

Later that summer, Tom sold his company. This explained the high multiplier they had offered us: had they possessed our molecular interaction technology as part of their portfolio, they would have been able to secure a much better price.

That day taught me something very important: that money doesn't drive me. I don't want to be a multi-millionaire. Rather, I want to build something that lasts – that's what drives me the most. I want to build a profitable business that lasts. And I want to do it my way: the way of the Honorable Entrepreneur.

Summary

My personal shift moment

Between 2010 and 2014, I transitioned from being a founder to being a real leader, paying the price for every lesson along the way. We grew fast. And I grew up. I had thought that founding a company was the hard part – it wasn't. Learning to lead people is what nearly broke me. Those years were brutal. But they were also the making of me, because I finally understood that building a company isn't about the tech, it's about the people who choose to build it with you.

- I pushed early team members too hard, failed to appreciate them, and watched most of them leave. It hurt, and I learned that leadership is earned, not assumed.

- We made hiring our craft and found nine key people who have become the "living hearts" of NanoTemper: they are our culture.

- We made our first acquisition – SAW Instruments in Bonn. This taught us that buying is easy, but the real challenge involves integrating cultures.

- We turned down an acquisition offer of 60 million dollars, because we were building something bigger than just a price tag.

Over this period, NanoTemper grew from three to 59 employees. Revenue jumped from 1 million to 11.7 million euros per year. And we expanded into the US and China. But the real shift occurred when I stopped being a builder of prototypes and started becoming a builder of people and principles.

How this chapter lives the Code of Honor

I build trust – or I build nothing

When a team member faked customer results, I let her go. We cried, but I couldn't save her while losing NanoTemper. In biotech, trust isn't just nice to have – it's everything. Lose it once, and it's gone for good.

I put people first – always

I regret not doing this at the start. I yelled at Hüseyin, underestimated Iman, and pushed too hard in a windowless lab. Most left – and I don't blame them. That pain taught me that leadership means lifting people up, not wearing them down. The ones who stayed became the heart of NanoTemper.

I scale smart and fast

We didn't wait for someone else to open up the US market. We shipped our first production instrument bound up by duct tape, built trust locally, and hired great people on the ground. We scaled country by country: with purpose, not with hype.

I build a profitable business that lasts

We stopped charging based on cost and started charging based on value. From 20,000 euros to 90,000 euros per instrument – that margin was our freedom. Profit let us grow without pressure from outsiders.

I execute my vision

We left the university basement, took bold pricing risks, and launched in the US with duct-taped hardware. We didn't wait for permission. We acted even when it felt insane to do so.

NOW OVER TO YOU

Leadership isn't about your title. It's about who you become when things fall apart. It's about the people you protect, and the trust you refuse to break, even when it hurts. You will fail. You will regret things. But if you lead with humility, stay curious, and put your mission above your pride, you'll become the kind of leader others want to follow.

A CHALLENGE FOR YOU

Look at your team. Who are the people you'd bet your company on? Write them down, take really good care of them, and update this list every year.

4: SCALING STRONG AND SMART – FROM THE ASHES TO STRATEGIC LEADER

S caling isn't just about hiring more people or selling more products – it's about making the right moves at the right time.

We nearly lost our momentum. We nearly crashed by growing too fast. And we almost got disrupted – until we disrupted ourselves first.

KILL YOUR COMPANY

The transformation started at the BioM CEO Christmas dinner in Munich, a "must-attend" event for all members of the local biotech scene. A former IBM R&D director delivered a keynote talk that changed everything for me. It was the first time that I had heard of the "kill the company" approach, from Lisa Bodell's 2012 book *Kill the Company: End the Status Quo, Start an Innovation Revolution*.

The talk focused on how to open your mind, genuinely understand what your customers need, and then apply this knowledge in practice. He said:

"People don't want lawnmowers. They want grass that stays short. If someone invents self-regulating grass, lawnmowers become irrelevant."

That was eye-opening for me. I bought the book, read half of it, then started putting one particular approach into action. What would a competitor have to build in order to kill NanoTemper? And, more importantly, why weren't we building that?

If there was to be a killer product, then this was precisely the product that we should be developing. Considering these questions unlocked something in me. It broadened my perspective and encouraged me to think big.

At the time, NanoTemper generated 100% of its revenue from a single product line: our biophysical Monolith instruments, based on our unique MicroScale Thermophoresis (MST) technology. These instruments relied on individual glass capillaries, however, which were delicate, manual, and incompatible with automation.

Now imagine a competitor launching an MST-compatible system that worked with 384-well plates – the gold standard for automation in labs. That would mean higher throughput, lower costs, and a longer walkaway time. It would destroy us: bye bye NanoTemper!

The problem was that back then, our theory suggested that MST would only work with thin glass capillaries, not with the thick wells of a plate. Everyone said that the latter would be impossible. But the "kill the company" approach was so inspiring to me that I was willing to challenge the impossible.

We hired Johannes and set him a single – bold – task: to invent a way to measure the molecular interactions in 384-well plates.

After engaging a team, what followed was five years of frustration, persistence, and eventual breakthrough. Our team succeeded. The result was our Dianthus instrument, which now holds the world record for the fastest biophysical screening technology. It can measure 1 million drug candidates in just four days.

JUMP: FROM STARTUP TO SCALING UP

At the start, our one invention had a single target market: basic research and early drug discovery. That's a typical beginning for a technology-driven startup. But for many, it's also where the story ends.

Commercial success involves delivering what customers want and need. Customers and markets evolve over time. Trends come and go. The right product at the right time can lead to success. However, you'll need more than one arrow in your quiver in order to adapt to future needs and trends. To move from startup to scaling up, you'll have to diversify your technology and product portfolio to move beyond trends and become more than a one-hit wonder.

Another turning point had its origins in an unexpected place: Ireland. No, not whisky – although I do enjoy that very much. It started in February 2014, with a strange email from Neil at University College Dublin. The subject? Urea – the compound in urine that denatures proteins. I bet you wish that it was whisky now!

Neil was using our Monolith NT.LabelFree instrument. But instead of using it to discover new protein-based drugs, the application we'd designed it for, he was instead using it to destroy proteins, combining them with urea in order to study chemical unfolding. My first thought when I read his email was: "What the f* * * does he want from me? What a strange application! Why isn't he using our instrument in the way we intended?"

But Neil was persistent. He explained that "Many of my colleagues would do the same. We just don't – because there's no instrument that lets us."

That caught my attention. An unmet need – a new market? I got excited and my mind started racing back and forth over the possibilities.

Neil's idea was that we should develop a special "Monolith NT.UREA" instrument for chemical stability studies of proteins. This prompted us to go on the road and talk with nine more customers working in the protein stability field.

The outcome wasn't exactly what Neil had wanted: we didn't do his thing with chemical unfolding and urea, and he didn't get a "Monolith NT.UREA" instrument. Our own small market study clearly indicated that there was significant potential for thermal stability studies of protein-based drugs. We developed a new technology called "nanoDSF" and an instrument named "Prometheus," which became our top seller. Six months after its launch, though, we also added chemical unfolding as a feature. Everyone was happy – especially Neil!

Thanks to Neil, we changed the game and took a customer-focused, market-driven approach. As a result, we stopped attempting to solve every problem with one type of technology, enabling us to adapt to various market needs, diversify our product offerings, and ultimately enter new markets. Furthermore, it also permitted us to parallelize our R&D. That's what you need to scale fast and smart.

The one thing that we kept fixed across our various technologies is that we fully focused on optical methods. By the end of 2024, we had nine optical methods over four different product lines: Monolith, Dianthus, Prometheus, and Andromeda. This shift, from solving problems with a single technology to designing market-driven solutions utilizing different technologies, allowed us to diversify, scale, and parallelize our R&D.

From then on, innovation became more than just something we did: it became our strategy.

INNOVATION AS A STRATEGY

Profitability allows you to take risks and invest in innovation. Innovative products yield higher margins and bigger profits. So profit fuels innovation and innovation fuels profit. At NanoTemper, our goal is to achieve over 20% profitability most years, in order to support both short-term growth and long-term moonshots.

The world changes. Your market shifts. Customers evolve. Competitors catch up. The only way to stay ahead is through better products. And that means innovation.

There are two kinds of innovation:

1. evolutionary (also known as continuous innovation); and
2. revolutionary (also known as disruptive innovation).

Everyone can and must conduct the first type: evolutionary innovation. It is something you can manage because you can set up processes for it, and it works well within teams.

By contrast, revolutionary innovation cannot be managed. It is achieved by individuals, by single inventors. You cannot predict and control it. The only thing you can do is increase its likelihood of occurring.

As an entrepreneur, you should master both types of innovation. You can delegate continuous innovation to your organization, so that you have more time for disruptive innovation. For example, your product managers can supervise the evolutionary innovation process. They constantly collect feedback from users and observe competitors, so, based on this, you can enhance the user experience and improve the features of your products and services. You won't win with this alone, but it will certainly keep you in the game. If your competitors make mistakes, it can even allow you to win.

Disruption is individual. At NanoTemper, we have two inventors who are able to create revolutionary innovations. The key is to have them working in the lab and to constantly expose them to new user problems, as disruption does not occur in a meeting room or brainstorming session – it happens on the lab bench.

The innovations are often so new that they can be difficult to understand when they are explained. At least, that's true for me! I need to see prototypes and observe the innovation "at work" to fully grasp it. Teamwork can stifle these innovations, as most team members will passionately argue why it can't work: it's just too novel and thus induces fear. But revolutionary innovation is an art: it can't be managed – it needs to be nurtured.

I don't know what our two inventors will invent next, or when. It could happen tomorrow or in seven years. But I know it will happen – if they have trust, freedom, and time.

This is how Andreas invented our new Spectral Shift technology, which is more than 10 times better than our old MST technology. It emerged from nothing, when Andreas discovered an artifact while working on a challenging experiment. I am confident that his invention will enable us to become the market leader in early drug discovery.

Another example is our world-record-holding Dianthus instrument, which I mentioned earlier. This took more than five years to create. It was often frustrating – like running a marathon, twice. For a long time, we got no results. We burned through a lot of resources, and the temptation to shift the focus to short-term wins was always there. Don't give in. If you stick with it, your reward will be more than a product. It will be market leadership. Innovation for impact requires time.

EARN THE MONEY BEFORE YOU SPEND IT

Having the best R&D team in the world and the most innovative products will get you nothing if no one buys them. Customers need to know about your products, and they must purchase them. That's why we've also invested heavily in sales and marketing. Marketing builds the brand and opens the door. Sales close the deal. There's often tension between these two teams – each wants credit for revenue. That's normal. Just remember, though: sales without marketing is hopeless, and marketing without sales is senseless.

We were still bootstrapped. We didn't have huge sums of VC or private equity investments in our bank accounts. We had to finance everything we did from our own revenues. We had to earn the money before we could spend it.

This meant that we first had to expand our sales force, then subsequently invest in the supply chain and production if we experienced an increase in demand. We had more than half of our staff in marketing, sales, and support to help scale the company.

Our typical sales cycle lasted for 213 days: it took a significant amount of time from the initial contact to a final purchase order. Consequently, our investments in operations followed our investments in sales, with a one-year delay.

Our strategy involved prioritizing sales first, then production, followed by sales again, then production once more – and continuing this cycle onward. It felt like a dance with a step frequency of a year. As a result, our supply chain and production teams often operated at or above 100% of their capacity, as we only invested further once we had earned the money. Yes, this created significant stress for these teams. Yes, we attempted other approaches – twice. Both times, however, these resulted in major layoffs. Always – really – keep your fixed costs, especially your salaries, under close control.

In our business, sales had to be local: you needed to be near the customer. In key markets, like the US, most of Europe, and China, we built our own direct salesforce. In smaller regions, like Australia, we worked through distributors.

Because sales were local, they were also territorial. And that made scaling complex. As founders, we saw a simple opportunity: if we weren't yet near market saturation, we could grow revenue by adding more salespeople. More people meant more ground covered and more deals closed. There was a clear path forward, at least for us, being the founders.

But for our salespeople, growth didn't feel like opportunity – it felt like pressure. Each time we added a new team member, each rep's territory got smaller. At the same time, we raised their targets: less ground but higher goals.

The pattern was clear: the more we scaled the team, the more each person had to hustle just to hit the same numbers. That tension was baked into the model. They had to work harder for each and every dollar. Many hated it. Over time, they either left or moved into leadership.

That's the nature of field sales. If your team feels like they're running on a treadmill, you're probably growing fast. We learned to expect it, and to support it. Strong recruiters were essential. So was a stable core of top performers who could anchor the team.

If someone asks me "What has NanoTemper done better than others?" my answer is often the following: "We invested more in growing our commercial team." As an entrepreneur, I saw it as my duty to earn money and bring innovations to the market, because I was sure that we provided important products that helped our customers to develop better therapies faster. During that time, I learned that innovating without selling was futile, and that business without innovation was hopeless.

HONORS, AWARDS, AND AWKWARD SITUATIONS

We had been very successful – a rare bootstrapped blossom in the garden of deep-tech startups. Our achievements didn't go unnoticed, especially in Germany. We received both the German Innovation Prize (Deutscher Innovationspreis) and the German Founders Award (Deutscher Gründerpreis).

The German Founders Award was especially memorable for me. The ceremony took place at the ZDF Hauptstadtstudio, one of Germany's major TV stations. Before the event started, I had a light-hearted chat with the moderator. She was from northern Bavaria, like me, and I naively shared a personal story with her. Guess what? During the live broadcast, she mentioned that story on national television. Ever since then, I've learned to approach all media conversations with intention: knowing exactly what I want to share and what I don't want to share.

But that wasn't the only awkward moment. The zipper of my trousers had broken just before the ceremony, and I couldn't close it properly. When they announced "And the winner is... NanoTemper," I couldn't leap up and celebrate in the way I wanted to – as I had to make sure that my zipper wasn't on display! In the video and all the official photos, you'll notice that I've carefully positioned myself to hide it.

Even so, it was an unforgettable evening. Stefan and I were proud, and so were our families, friends, and the entire NanoTemper team. It felt like a kind of knighthood.

Another proud moment came later in the year, when the German finance magazine *CAPITAL* named me as one of the Top 40 under 40, similar to the Forbes 30 under 30. It was the first time that I had been referred to as an entrepreneur, rather than just a founder or a CEO. That shift in title meant a lot to me.

The very first thing that happened after *CAPITAL* published the list? A call from a real estate agent in New York City: "Congratulations! Interested in investing in Manhattan property?" My colleagues Christian and Angela were sitting next to me and nearly fell off their chairs laughing. It was surreal!

But the best part of that honor wasn't the recognition – it was the network. The Top 40 under 40 community is incredibly active, with local meetups, WhatsApp and Discord groups, and an annual alumni event in Berlin, where we welcome the new generation of honorees. It remains one of the most inspiring and supportive networks that I'm part of.

THE VILLAGE BOY IS DEAD – A NEW GLOBAL ME IS BORN

As 2015 came to a close, I found myself at a crossroads: I felt stuck in old patterns, both personally and professionally, and a deep sense of unhappiness surrounded me. My marriage to my childhood sweetheart, from a neighboring village, which had lasted for nearly two decades, was coming to an end. I was grappling with the reality that even though I had grown beyond my origins, I was still emotionally tied to them. I realized that my past, my old self, was now holding me back. I saw two paths forward: to remain the nice village boy that I'd always been or to step into becoming someone new.

In early 2016, I made the difficult decision to separate from my wife and move out. It was a visible and public declaration of personal transformation. People who I had once considered close friends now turned their backs on me. I was walking away from my past – and my past was walking away from me. The weight of this change was overwhelming. I lost 16 kg in just three months. I couldn't eat. I couldn't sleep. My body changed, and my mind changed. There were moments when I felt completely alone. But in that emptiness, I found the space to imagine a new future.

It was an incredibly painful time – a time of tears: not just for me, but for everyone around me. I was so consumed by my personal change that I couldn't focus on the business for about a year. I was very fortunate: Stefan and our team carried NanoTemper through that period and stood by me throughout my emotional highs and lows. A stable business and personal crisis can be managed. But crises in both? That would've been too much!

Unsurprisingly, this period also marked a time of renewal. I rediscovered a love for sports that I hadn't felt since my PhD days. I started running along the river Isar twice a week – it became a ritual, one that helped me reconnect with myself and gain clarity. I hadn't realized just how much I'd missed it until I started doing it again. Running didn't just improve my fitness – it also cleared my mind.

The transformation went deeper than that, however. Most notably, I shifted from being introverted to being more open, curious, and engaged. I took English lessons so that I could communicate better – something the village boy had never taken seriously, since Stefan had handled most of our international business. I also embraced new habits: regular exercise, self care, and a stronger focus on personal and professional growth, which involved opening myself up to coaching for the very first time.

I never used to believe in coaching, but Daniel helped me to change my mind. His 360-degree feedback helped me to become a better leader. He interviewed key members of our team and provided me with a full analysis of how they saw me – I still tear up when I read it. I had always worried that people didn't respect me enough. However, the opposite turned out to be true: the team respected me so much that they felt intimidated by me – my communication style was also cornering people, without me even realizing it. That latter insight alone changed how I led, as well as who I became.

What's more, this period of transformation also freed me from a fear that I had carried from early childhood.

Up to 2016, I had major problems traveling, as a result of a childhood trauma that had shaped much of my adult life. When I was about two-and-a-half years old, I became seriously ill and had to stay in a hospital in Coburg. My parents weren't allowed to remain with me, so I spent the nights entirely alone. My mother later revealed to me that I would still be screaming when she returned in the morning. Those nights clearly left a deeply emotional mark on me.

This trauma accompanied me into adulthood and severely limited my ability to travel for business. Each night that I had to spend away from home was a struggle. The anxiety would start building up weeks in advance, making long-distance travel a stressful and exhausting experience. Given this, I mostly stayed tied to Munich, avoiding overnight trips whenever possible.

But when everything else changed, I finally found myself able to break free from the limitation. I learned to stay in different places, in different hotels, without fear. I even started to enjoy it! I felt that I was unlocking a new part of my life – and, with that, the whole world opened up to me.

I'm a fan of Greek mythology: my entire transformation was like a phoenix rising from the ashes. So please let me tell you this. You are not a victim of fate. You can take your future into your own hands. You just have to make it happen...

SEPARATED MANAGEMENT AND LEADERSHIP

As previously suggested, this personal transformation not only changed how I lived, but it also changed how I led. When I started showing up differently in my personal life, it soon became clear that Stefan and I would also need to rethink how we were showing up in the business. NanoTemper was growing rapidly, and our approach to leadership needed to evolve with it.

It had taken us seven years to grow from two founders to a mid-sized company of 75 people, but during the period from 2015 to 2019, our team more than doubled, meaning we had 167 employees. The risks we took as well as our continuous – and disruptive – innovations had paid off.

In order to achieve this growth, Stefan and I had to adapt our management style. We clearly defined our responsibilities and accountabilities. We both valued independence, freedom, and quick decisions – discussing each decision and mutually agreeing on the way forward didn't align with our personal preferences at the time.

We decided to split NanoTemper into two parts: Stefan would lead the commercial side, while I would lead the technical side. This way, we could manage NanoTemper's rapid growth effectively. As we had doubled the number of employees, the split we implemented meant that we would only have to manage – and lead – half of our people each. It also felt satisfying, as we could each focus on our areas of expertise.

We had significant success following this approach: we only needed to coordinate every few weeks, to discuss the major goals and overall strategy. It also meant that we were very fast: if you don't have to discuss every decision, you can make a decision more quickly – often, I would only need a few data points and my gut feeling before taking action. I made a lot of mistakes this way, but I could also correct them speedily. This arrangement was especially beneficial for me, as it allowed me to cope with my personal issues during a difficult time.

During this four-year period, we increased our annual revenue from 15.7 million euros to 31.8 million euros. We expanded globally, establishing offices in San Francisco, Boston, Krakow, London, Shanghai, Beijing, and Tokyo. We also launched operations in South America, Australia, the Middle East, and even Africa. Additionally, we developed new optical technologies called TRIC, nanoDSF, backreflection, Dynamic Light Scattering (DLS), and Static Light Scattering (SLS), plus we also invented a method for measuring in multiwell plates (some of which have already been discussed).

When you look at the financial key performance indicators (KPIs), you can see that this was an outstanding period for us. Sharply separating our responsibilities and accountabilities reduced complexity and enabled us to make bold moves quickly: exactly what you need to do to scale your company. As you'll read next, our financial success was also noticed by the big players in our industry.

Although the clear division of responsibilities between Stefan and myself had had a positive impact, it also hindered our growth after 2019. Years later, we hit upon a new solution. This is a general pattern: structures and strategies only work effectively for a certain period of time, at a certain stage of your company. Just because something worked well in the past doesn't mean that it will continue to work well in the future. You need to develop an understanding and a feeling for when to change.

My indicator of a necessary change at NanoTemper is when I observe increasing friction and conflict across our entire company over a period of several months. Whenever I notice this, I listen very carefully to the members of our organization. Most of the time, increasing our efficiency and improving our existing structures and processes is sufficient.

Every four to five years, however, a major change is necessary: you must dismantle whole departments and structures and then rebuild them. You'll read more about that in the next section...

THE ULTIMATE TEMPTATION

NanoTemper's rapid growth had caught the attention of nearly every major player in the industry, so it was only a matter of time before someone made us an offer.

I have already hinted at the moment in the book's introduction – the email that arrived on a quiet Sunday evening, shaking everything that I thought that I wanted. The amount was staggering. The kind of life-changing money that most people can't even imagine. But instead of excitement, I felt something else entirely.

Saying yes would have changed everything: the company we'd built, the team who'd believed in us, the independence we'd fought for – it would all be gone, just like that. I had spent years proving that rapid growth and profitability could go hand in hand – was I now ready to hand it all over?

The offer would have meant more than a hundred million dollars for me personally – an unbelievable number for someone from a small village in Bavaria, the son of a kindergarten nurse and an electrician.

To put this into context, this same "Big Company" acquired a similarly sized competitor for 1.4 billion dollars not long afterward.

Their proposal to us wasn't just about the money, though – it also came with all the right promises. They wanted to make NanoTemper their global "Center of Excellence in Protein Characterization and Bio-Molecular Interactions," keeping our headquarters in Munich and giving us the freedom to operate independently. They emphasized their long-term commitment and offered access to expanded commercial resources, strategic marketing, and technical support. On paper, it looked ideal...

But the more I thought about it, the more uneasy I felt. Selling didn't excite me. It felt wrong. It would have gone against everything I stood for – my Code of Honor. Would you sell your "baby" for the right price?

I didn't want to cash out – I wanted to build further, to scale to a hundred million dollars in revenue, on our terms, with our culture, and with our mission intact. I wanted to develop products that could help to create better therapies more quickly. I wanted to have an impact and grow responsibly. And I wanted to achieve this *with* NanoTemper.

NanoTemper's best-in-class growth continued. In the years that followed, other offers came in. Each one was politely declined. NanoTemper's independence was no longer a question – it was a choice.

THE WORST DAY OF MY BUSINESS LIFE

Despite our success, in 2019 we found that we had overextended ourselves. We'd expanded the R&D team, hired aggressively, and even ventured into AI – too early. That year, business started slow. Month after month, revenues stayed below expectations. Projections warned of serious cash flow problems within six to nine months.

We had made financial mistakes and lost control over our costs – especially fixed costs, like salaries. Fixed costs are the worst kind to have to deal with in a crisis. We were betting on rising revenue. Instead, revenue shrank. We'd broken our own rule, by spending money we hadn't yet earned. It was clear: we had to cut salary costs – and fast.

Severance costs are expensive, and it takes time – often six months or so – before savings show up. If you want lower costs by December, you need to act in June. Our salary costs were nearly 2 million euros too high, so we had no time to waste.

Together with our leadership team, we reviewed every role and performance record. It was brutal but necessary. High salaries and low performance – we couldn't afford both. In the end, 19 people had to go.

This wasn't just about the numbers – it was about survival, for everyone else and indeed for NanoTemper itself. But that didn't make it any easier. I had many sleepless nights and got my first gray hairs – it shaped me forever.

You can't lay off 10% of your team without consequences. If it's mishandled, it destroys the culture for years. People start wondering "Am I next?" And no one does their best work when feeling fear. It's your duty as a leader to create safety, especially during a crisis.

We made a plan: all conversations would occur within 24 hours – and once they were done, they were done. We promised there would be no more layoffs. To keep that promise, we cut a little deeper than we needed to, building in a buffer to protect trust.

Stefan and I handled every single conversation ourselves. We explained our reasons, expressed our gratitude, and honored what each person had contributed to the company. It was the hottest week of the year, in the summer of 2019. The different time zones only made it harder. From Wednesday night to Thursday night, we held deeply emotional conversations for 24 hours nonstop.

It was the worst day of my business life. Why? Because it was down to me. I had hired too fast, and too soon, before the revenue was there. I had broken my own rule: I had hoped, speculated, and believed – and I had been wrong.

I promised myself that I'd never make that mistake again. That's how deep it went. But now I knew for sure: profit first, optimism second. (Spoiler alert: I did make that mistake again, in 2022–2023, when optimism got the better of me once more...)

Back in 2019, though, those painful cuts proved prescient. When Covid-19 hit in 2020, we were lean, focused, and ready. The worst day of my business life had in fact prepared us for one of the hardest periods that the world would ever face.

SUMMARY

MY PERSONAL SHIFT MOMENT

During the years 2014 to 2019, I stopped being just a builder and became a strategic leader. But the real transformation went deeper than strategy.

- I stopped micromanaging and let our inventors lead. That trust gave birth to the breakthroughs that led to our Dianthus and Prometheus product lines.

- I broke free from old fears, rediscovered my strengths, embraced coaching, and became the leader my team needed.

- I over-hired and overestimated our growth. The result was 19 layoffs in 24 hours. It was my worst day as a leader, but it saved the company.

- I learned to separate management from leadership. Stefan and I split our responsibilities between us, doubled our team, and led the company's expansion across three continents.

NanoTemper's revenue grew from 11.7 million euros per year to 31.8 million euros per year, while our headcount increased from 59 to 167 employees.

We launched in new markets, opened offices across three continents, and turned innovation into our flywheel. But this isn't just a story about scaling – it's also a story about letting go, about assumptions, about people, about past versions of myself, and about growing up as a leader.

HOW THIS CHAPTER LIVES THE CODE OF HONOR

I build trust – or I build nothing

We cut 19 roles and held each difficult conversation ourselves. No emails. No shortcuts. Just honest face-to-face talks. Trust isn't built in the good times – it's built in the hard talks that you'd rather avoid.

I put people first – always

Even when I could barely lead myself, my team didn't waver. Later, I showed up differently: open to feedback, ready for coaching, and attempting to be deeply human. People didn't just stay because of our vision – they stayed because we changed together.

I innovate for impact

Our entire business once depended on tiny glass tubes: fragile, manual, and impossible to scale. Then I asked a question no founder wants to face: "How could a competitor destroy us?" That fear became our fuel. We challenged our own technology and broke our own rules. Five years later, Dianthus was born, the world's fastest screening platform. Innovation isn't comfort – it's confrontation.

I scale smart and fast

We scaled like a pendulum: sales first, then production, then sales again, then production again. We only spent what we'd earned. We followed demand, not ego. It wasn't glamorous, but it worked. And when we broke that rhythm? The layoffs hit hard. Smart scaling isn't about speed – it's about sequence.

I build a profitable business that lasts

A hundred million dollars on the table. Just for me... A very tempting offer to acquire NanoTemper. But why sell a profitable business for a one-time sum when your team is only just beginning to make a long-term impact? Profit gave us a choice. Purpose made the decision easy.

I execute my vision

I stopped leading with invention and started leading with intention. We stopped asking "What else can we do with this one technology?" and started asking "What else do our customers need?" That shift turned NanoTemper from a one-hit wonder into a portfolio company, with various technologies designed to solve real problems across the entire drug development journey.

NOW OVER TO YOU

You can't scale your company until you scale yourself. That means letting go of who you were – and growing into who your team needs you to be.

Sometimes this means trusting others to lead. Sometimes it means confronting your own blind spots. And sometimes it means saying no to a hundred million dollars: because you're building something money just can't buy.

You'll make painful mistakes. You'll experience moments that shake your confidence. But if you stay honest, stay learning, and lead with courage, you'll come out stronger. Not only as a better entrepreneur, but also as a better human being.

CHALLENGE FOR YOU

What's one fear, or habit, that you know you need to let go of to grow as a leader? Write down how you can overcome it. And then start to do that now.

PHILIPP BAASKE

5: BREAKING BOTTLENECKS – FROM STARTUP TO GLOBAL FORCE

It was a Sunday in San Francisco – 5:43 p.m. local time on 12 January 2020. Everything was as it always was. I arrived on a Lufthansa Airbus and then faced the usual challenge: the endless line at border control. I spent 140 minutes standing alongside passengers from Munich as well as Wuhan, China. Two weeks later, we all knew about Wuhan. Three weeks later, all flights from China to the US were canceled. Luckily, I didn't catch Covid-19 then.

It was a wild time. A pandemic in the modern era unleashed real-time madness across all the social media channels. It was unclear what would happen next and what actions we should take – it was exactly the time for effective leadership.

LEADERSHIP DURING THE PANDEMIC

In 2020, Stefan and I were managing NanoTemper as co-CEOs with strictly separated responsibilities – Stefan was leading the commercial departments, like sales and marketing, while I was leading the technical ones, like R&D and production. We were working closely with Hans-Jürgen, our Chief Technology Officer. Hans-Jürgen is exactly 19 years and 364 days older than I am, and he was previously the CEO of our capillary supplier. More importantly, though, he had also been the Chairman of the board of the German Red Cross (DRK) in his hometown for decades, and thus he was also a leader when it came to disaster control. In Germany, if there is a catastrophe, you call the DRK to handle it.

Ever since I first met Hans-Jürgen, in 2007, he has been a role model and mentor for me: not only did his experience and calmness in disaster relief operations significantly aid us, but it also provided us with emotional safety – and the confidence required to lead ourselves through this crisis.

Our first step was to establish a daily routine: we met for an hour every day at 7:30 a.m., before most of our people started working. We updated each other, tried to understand (as far as we could) the current situation with the pandemic, then discussed what and how we ought to communicate to our employees. We aimed to stay ahead of the wave and offer a safe harbor for our people amid the ongoing storm of conflicting information. Indeed, we agreed that it was better to say nothing at all than to further confuse matters with incorrect facts. This, along with our daily routine, helped me a lot: like everyone else, I was feeling insecure and afraid of what would come next.

We defined a source of truth to follow: the Bavarian State. We used the information and rules it published to guide NanoTemper through the crisis, reading what they suggested, discussing it, and then choosing whether or not to put it into action.

For our internal communications, we always announced in advance when we were intending to publish new guidelines or rules. Whenever we had to shift our timelines, we also informed everyone as soon as possible: doing so, or simply stating that we weren't able to say anything until a certain time, helped our people a lot – it generated trust.

Trust is a quality that needs to be actively nurtured, because if your team loses faith in your leadership, you will lose the game. Once you gain their trust and demonstrate to them your dedication, that's when you can lead effectively. Only then will your team be ready to follow you – and only then will you be able to take action, navigate the crisis, and endure.

LEADING WITH INTEGRITY – TRUST BEATS CASH

The first lockdown directly impacted our revenues, dropping them sharply. Universities were shut, meaning that one of our most important customer groups simply vanished overnight, with orders coming to a stop. March and April 2020 were some of the weakest months that we'd experienced in a long time. Like every company facing uncertainty, we started thinking through various scenarios. We knew we had to act responsibly, with our people, our cash flow, and our values in mind.

One option on the table was "Kurzarbeit" – short-term work, a program that the German government strongly supported at the time. It was widely taken up – and for many, it proved to be a practical way to stabilize cash flow. Our supply chain and production teams had little to do during lockdown, so, technically, we could have applied for support on that basis. More cash is always helpful, especially in times of global uncertainty. But even though we qualified under the rules, it felt like we would be taking advantage of it – quite frankly, it felt like it would be fraud. As it was against our values, we didn't do it. I know other companies made different choices. They took the money while expecting their teams to work full time: their employees saw through it, people talked, and it ended up damaging trust. In some cases, those companies no longer exist, or they've been absorbed into others.

While our supply chain and production teams remained quiet, our other departments were under intense pressure. R&D and sales, for instance, were busier than ever: biotechnology was poised to save the world with diagnostics, PCR had become a household term, and mRNA vaccines were being developed at lightning speed. Many institutes and companies were working on therapeutics, and our instruments were part of that. NanoTemper's technology was featured in press releases across the industry, including ones from BioNTech and Pfizer. Our teams were working flat out, pushing forward, and proud to be part of something that mattered.

Although there was a worldwide crisis during the first few months of the Covid-19 pandemic, which impacted many industries for two years, it ended up being a boom time for us. Governments all over the world were investing billions of dollars into diagnostics, therapies, and vaccines.

We noticed the change in June 2020, when the pandemic prompted an unexpected surge in demand for our biophysical instruments – just as our once-reliable supply chains were beginning to falter. Overnight, operational excellence ceased to be a nice-to-have and instead became our lifeline. If we didn't master it, we risked missing this boom – and, worse, losing the trust of the customers who depended on us.

At this time, we quickly realized that we needed someone to steer our operations. Finding that person wasn't easy: it took us three attempts to come across the right fit – someone who understood our pace, culture, and ambitions. That's the reality of hiring for a brand-new role: you may need to learn what you truly need and what kind of leader can thrive in your world.

To put this brand-new role into context, consider how much we'd grown. In 2010, NanoTemper was shipping fewer than 30 instruments and a few hundred consumable kits each year. By mid-2020, we were building eight complex instruments each week and moving over 2,000 consumable kits each month. Without a solid operational system – covering the flow of information, materials, and cash from purchase through to production, quality control, sales, and support – we would burn our money and reputation just as fast as we were growing.

That's why we adopted two core principles. First, we mapped our end-to-end process, borrowing from the automotive industry's "lean production" to eliminate waste at each step. Second, we tied our day-to-day work back to our long-term strategy by rolling out Objectives and Key Results (OKRs), a goal-setting framework that had been championed at Intel and popularized by Google. Jocelyn, our US-based Head of Marketing, first introduced us to OKRs: she understood their power because she'd lived in the Bay area, which was steeped in that culture.

With help from consultants Ilka and Marco, we set quarterly OKRs, which forced us to pause, align, and reset every three months. Anna, Gernot, Christian, and their teams took us from being a "more poor than good" operation to becoming one of the fastest in our industry, without ever sacrificing quality. They slashed our lead time from seven weeks to just 48 hours! That's operational excellence in action.

Why obsess over speed? Many of our customers are VC-backed biotech startups racing against the clock. When the funding arrives, time literally costs them millions. They'll take the first instrument they can get – so if you can deliver in 48 hours, you win.

I understand why deep-tech founders roll their eyes at operations: it feels tedious compared to inventing the next breakthrough. But this is the secret: smooth operations will become your cash cow and all that work will pay off for you. With the right team running the engine, you stop fighting daily fires, freeing you to think big, sharpen strategy, and scale faster. However, that operational strength was soon tested by an unexpected move from a familiar competitor...

SECOND-MOVER STRATEGY FOR MARKET DOMINANCE

Our Prometheus instrument, built on our innovative nanoDSF technology (a method for measuring the stability of biotherapeutics), was not only a visible outcome of our transition from being a "one-hit-wonder" startup to becoming a multi-tech scale-up, but it also became our best seller. One of the largest biotechnology companies even referred to it as the "new gold standard" in our industry. We were very proud and I thought that we were the best – which I now know is dangerous thinking. That mistake led me to become arrogant and lazy. But not for long...

Tom, the guy who had tried to acquire us for 60 million dollars in 2014, had since built a new company that was strongly backed by private equity funding. This new company grew very quickly, as they purchased company after company and technology after technology. They integrated these into their product portfolio and launched them on the market with a strong sales force. In marketing and sales, I'm always learning a lot from Tom – he is a genius at positioning his companies.

Tom's new company already had an alternative to our Prometheus instrument in their product portfolio, although ours easily outperformed theirs. Tom also knew this, so he acquired a UK-based company and added two new technologies to the product – optical technologies called DLS and SLS. When he did this, our product was no longer the best: they now had three technologies in their device, while we only had one. More importantly, with DLS and SLS, they provided the technologies that customers needed to meet the requirements of the Food and Drug Administration (FDA) for measuring aggregates. We had to react to compete with them – and, as you might guess, I woke up, developed a plan, and executed it boldly.

We also decided to add optical technologies for measuring aggregates to Prometheus. First, we attempted to develop an alternative to DLS and SLS, to ensure our uniqueness. We tried Fluorescence Anisotropy. This optical technology would have enabled us to measure a wider range of concentrations of biotherapeutics than is possible with DLS and SLS, therefore giving us a strong advantage. But we failed with it – and we lost valuable time. We were finding sales increasingly difficult to make, plus we were losing market share to Tom's new company. Now we were running out of time!

Then we went all in. We began to develop our own innovative DLS and SLS technology, a 100% digital solution, while Tom's company only had an old-fashioned analog version. No one had ever applied DLS and SLS to our very thin capillary sample format – again, another new invention. We initiated the development project with an interdisciplinary product team of six people, keeping it small and agile. In just six months, this team created prototypes and tested them with customers, proving that our approach would work in the field.

Empowered by this early success, we later put 37 people on the project, utilizing 90% of our R&D resources. Not everyone – but everyone who could help to move this new product forward quickly. Just 11 months later, we launched the production instrument Prometheus Panta – even the pandemic couldn't stop us! This is now our most important product, and we've nearly pushed Tom out of the European market. I was waiting for him to react but knew we'd be ready.

This experience triggered me to develop a "second-mover strategy."

Most of our competitors are based in the US and funded by private equity, so many new trends emerge there first. The US-based FDA makes the rules and sets the pace, before other countries follow. This means that our well-funded and well-connected – and mostly US-based – competition can recognize new markets ahead of us, then quickly acquire companies and technologies to dominate these markets. This is a powerful first-mover strategy.

Our competitors work incredibly fast, at what sometimes seems like supersonic speed, but they are driven solely by short-term financial and operational goals, so they often neglect R&D and customer support. The R&D personnel tend to leave or are laid off shortly after each acquisition, as the company is simply aiming to maximize its profitability. This provides us with the opportunity to outcompete them over time.

So, my second-mover strategy is:

1. to follow closely what companies they acquire and for which markets;
2. to understand if their new products bring real value to customers;
3. to develop and launch a slightly better product within 18 months;
4. to continuously improve this product with strong R&D; and
5. to invest strongly in customer support and customer relationships.

By doing this, we can gradually increase our market share. This approach is particularly effective against mid-sized VC- and private-equity-funded competitors. We executed this strategy very successfully with our Prometheus Panta instrument line, and we have also started doing so with our Dianthus product family.

For our competitors, customer support is often viewed merely as a cost, so its impact is widely underestimated and it is therefore neglected. I see things differently, however: customer support as well as your entire customer relationship management strategy are among the most crucial elements for lasting success, and they therefore constitute a central aspect of this second-mover strategy.

I've experienced this over time: not only does it ultimately return what you've invested many times over, but your dedicated support team members often turn out to be your hidden superstars. Your customers appreciate it when you're there for them after they've purchased your product. They share their experiences with their peers in other companies, becoming your strongest advocates – and this is the best marketing for you.

These customers are also likely to buy the next generation of your products. One of the best compliments I've ever received came from a competing sales representative: "Your customers are so loyal to you – when we see someone with your products, we know he's lost to us." This means that our customers trust us – and trust is the currency for building a lasting business.

This whole experience with our second-mover approach showed me something important: you can have the smartest strategy and the best product, but if your people don't really get it, then nothing happens. They need to clearly understand what it is that you're aiming for, believe that it's achievable, and then actually want to make it happen. Indeed, it was then that I realized that getting the communication right, building trust, and living our values were just as crucial as technical innovation. And that's why I began focusing on culture and communication.

THE POWER OF CULTURE AND COMMUNICATION

Goals and strategies must evolve as markets shift. In 2021, we set some new financial targets: a hundred million euros in annual revenue and 20% profitability (EBITDA – earnings before interest, taxes, depreciation, and amortization) by 2030.

Even so, I realized that I needed a vision that would transcend spreadsheets – a rallying cry that would tap into people's hearts. When your team grows way past triple digits, spread across continents and time zones, clear communication isn't just helpful – it's critical. You must ensure that everyone understands where you're headed, why you chose that destination, and how you plan to get there.

Once I saw how powerfully such a message could unite the whole team, I hired one of Germany's top speaking coaches to help me hone my delivery. He taught me three things.

First, to speak in funnels – also called "inverse pyramids" – like former US president Barack Obama, by utilizing a communication style that starts out broad then narrows down, moving from big-picture themes and values toward specific actions and takeaways.

Second, to speak like a leader instead of a scientist, by focusing on the main message instead of the details.

And third, to focus on my audience and their needs, rather than on me – on my technology and my company.

It all sounds simple, right? In any case, this shift in my approach had a massive impact. Instead of standing before people who preferred to play with their smartphones rather than listen to me, I started to receive standing ovations following my talks!

I then took this learning and applied it to team communication. When we first unveiled our goal of a hundred million euros in revenue, we were met with skeptical faces. That sounded impossible! But Stefan and I refused to let the target go. I realized that a compelling vision of ambitious goals only takes root when you repeat it, again and again. So we spoke about this vision at every meeting, at every town hall, and even during every hallway conversation.

After three months of relentless repetition, the team didn't just accept the goal, they also started claiming it as their own. We realized that something had shifted when our team members (such as Tobias) started coming forward with their suggestions as to how the company could hit a hundred million euros in revenue by 2029. This revealed to me that true communication means saying the same thing until you can no longer hear it yourself.

As this suggests, culture is not what you display on a company intranet – it's what happens when no one's watching. At NanoTemper, we distilled our values into three guiding principles: trusting collaboration, customer-focused impact, and fearless curiosity. The real test would involve daily behavior...

I still remember this... Karolina, one of our most promising leaders, arranged a meeting to plan a voice of customer study for a new market. She asked five experienced leaders – including me – to participate and did an excellent job of inviting us, by providing a clear agenda as well as a strong to-do list, so that everyone would be well prepared.

When we started the virtual meeting, everyone had their cameras on. Karolina was very present, her eyes focused straight on the camera lens.

But then Ralf, another of the leaders, could be seen lounging in his chair, before almost sliding off it. He seemed unfocused. Karolina explained her topic and guided us through the accompanying slide deck. It was a very important topic, because it was about entering a big new market. But suddenly, I couldn't believe what I was seeing: Ralf took a call on his smartphone while Karolina was speaking. My anger surged – what disrespectful behavior!

After her presentation, Karolina addressed each one of us individually, going over our to-dos. When she reached Ralf, he unmuted his microphone and started speaking in a provocative tone of voice: "Sorry, I haven't listened – what did you say?" Karolina remained calm and repeated her question. Ralf then replied even more provocatively: "Sorry, which email?" But I knew he had received this email, as he had discussed it with me. I was on the verge of exploding in anger – it was difficult to maintain control: one of our leaders, who should be a role model, displaying such disrespect. Unbelievable! Unacceptable!

After I calmed myself down, I sent Ralf a short message: "Your behavior in this meeting was unacceptable. You showed a complete lack of respect for Karolina. I expect you to apologize to her immediately."

A week later, I had a one-on-one meeting with Karolina. At the end of the meeting, Karolina said "Philipp, there is one more thing. Ralf apologized to me. I have been in business for over 30 years now. I've never experienced a situation where one of my bosses stopped another from treating me without respect. I want to thank you for this." She had tears in her eyes as she said this – it meant a lot to her. And her feedback still means a lot to me.

When you stand up for your people and your principles, you build trust. Indeed, trust is the backbone of any high-performing team. It turns visions into lived reality and goals into shared ownership. In today's fast-moving biotech world, where customers demand tools within 48 hours and VC-backed startups race against the clock, culture and communication become your ultimate competitive edge.

You can master every operational metric, but without a culture that can rally behind a clear vision and a leader who can communicate relentlessly, you'll never sustain momentum. Conversely, when people feel heard, respected, and inspired to contribute, you unlock the true power of your organization – and you set the stage for breakthroughs that not only hit targets, but also change lives.

Building a strong culture with clear communication is crucial. But even these are tested when rapid growth pushes your organization into moments of profound change – moments I call revolutions.

EVOLUTION UNTIL REVOLUTION: FAST GROWTH EATS THE PAST FOR BREAKFAST

Thanks to our operational excellence and second-mover strategy, we could grow and scale fast. When you scale fast, everything you build – structures, processes, and culture – becomes outdated just as your team is beginning to get comfortable. Hypergrowth is an operation on the beating heart of your company, with no anesthesia – and no pause button.

Most of the time, this feels like an evolution. Every few years, it becomes a revolution. And every revolution has its victims.

We learned this the hard way, initially in product management. At one point, we had 10 people in the team – far too many for our size at the time. We trusted our Chief Product Officer and gave her a year to fix it. But things got worse, so we parted ways. Eventually, we made a tough call: we shut the entire team down, from 10 people to zero. For six months, we had no product management at all. Then we rebuilt it from scratch, with just three new hires. Within months, they delivered more than the 10 people had done before. This is what revolution looks like: bold, painful, and necessary.

The hard truth is that when you grow fast, by 30% or more over a year, you will lose 20%–30% of your team every three to five years. Some people leave because they miss the "small company" feel or yearn for a version of the company that no longer exists – they can't let go of the past. And if you're not willing to let them go, you'll get stuck, too.

I've had to part ways with friends – with people who helped us build our foundations. It hurt every time, but I've never regretted it.

Scale demands specialization. In the beginning, you hire generalists who wear five hats. But as you grow, you bring in specialists: people who can outperform the generalists in every domain. The generalists face a choice: specialize, lead, stay general (if there's space), or leave. Some will adapt, but most won't.

Even fewer make it through multiple revolutions. I believe that less than 5% of early-stage team members can grow through more than three major transitions. That includes the founders. I later realized I was one of them.

From the end of 2019 until 2021, we were constantly hitting a wall. We felt stuck: leading and managing NanoTemper based on our gut feelings was hindering our growth.

I'd sensed that something was wrong for a couple of years. I felt that I needed to change, but I wasn't ready or willing to accept that. I'd blindfolded myself, going through the motions of the busy daily grind and constantly fighting fires, without seeing the big picture. The business was doing well:

why change a well-functioning system? And yet there was still a feeling that something was amiss…

Then, one day, Jocelyn said the following directly to our faces: "Stefan and Philipp, you are the bottleneck. You hinder us to grow." For a few seconds, I hated her for saying this. But once my ego stopped screaming and my accompanying anger faded, I realized that she was right. You are very lucky when someone in your company trusts you enough to tell you the truth: that's the feedback you need to hear in order to grow – as a company and as a leader.

The truth was that our previously successful management style, which had divided NanoTemper into two parts, each being governed by one of us, no longer worked. We had to tear down the wall that we had built between the two silos: commercial and technical. It was time for another revolution.

This is what we needed for our next step:

A) a system for steering the company, instead of relying on our gut feelings;
B) a new type of leadership and management style;
C) an executive management team to lead;
D) a clear mission, vision, strategy, and goals; and
E) a holistic communication channel.

For everyone except us, it seemed obvious that these changes had to be made. Shortly after we had implemented them, an employee from our production team approached me and said "What took you so long?"

Here's the thing: when you're in the system, it's hard to see that you're part of the problem. The input from Jocelyn, from her different perspective, opened my eyes.

Once Jocelyn had helped us to see the path forward, Stefan and I didn't waste a moment. We merged our separate roles into a single Founders Team – two people speaking with one voice – and dove straight into joint decision-making. Each of our strategy sessions and meetings now involved shared responsibility: it was challenging, but that unity laid the foundation for lasting change.

After that, we built a new leadership layer: an Executive Team reporting directly to us, supported by a cross-functional group of People Leaders drawn from our department heads and team leads. Those first few years were rocky: we cycled through nearly every Executive Team member at least once before finding the right mix, but our persistence ultimately paid off. We eventually settled into a streamlined reporting flow: team members to team leaders to department heads to executives to founders. That helped to keep our hierarchy as flat as possible while also ensuring clear accountability.

As someone who thrives on innovation, I've never loved rigid processes accompanied by endless documentation. Even so, I understood that operational excellence was non-negotiable if NanoTemper was to scale. Handing these tasks over to people who excel at them freed Stefan and I to focus on our true passion: defining the company's long-term vision, crafting its strategy, and driving its execution.

Do you remember Götz Werner's statement that founders grow by sharing responsibilities? That's exactly what we did here: we handed over the responsibility for the daily business and all its operations to our new Executive Team.

This transition was extremely challenging: it was difficult for me to relinquish my dictatorship over my technical kingdom, let alone share and democratize it. I was in conflict with my ego. However, as the owner of NanoTemper, I realized that a new structure would be far better for the growth of the company. This struggle taught me a great deal about myself. Scaling systems was hard. But what about scaling myself? Even harder... Still, that's a cornerstone in my journey of becoming an Honorable Entrepreneur.

Summary

My personal shift moment

Between 2020 and 2023, I stopped managing by instinct and started leading by design. However, this shift went deeper than tools and systems: it ended up changing me.

- I went from being a reactive firefighter to a structured visionary. The pandemic forced clarity. My daily crisis calls at 7:30 a.m. taught me what calm and decisive leadership looks like.

- I stopped resisting structure and started embracing operational excellence. I finally stepped outside the system and saw the wall I'd helped build. When Jocelyn said "You two are the bottleneck," it hurt, but she was right — and that truth set us free.

- I let go of my kingdom: no more silos and no more split leadership. We built one executive team, one reporting line, one direction — all together.

- I discovered the real power of communication: not by giving one great speech but by having a communication strategy and walking the talk, enabling everyone to understand and then follow me.

NanoTemper grew from 31.8 million euros to 56 million euros in revenue, and to 229 team members.

We restructured, launched new products, transformed operations, and became a truly global player – but this wasn't just about scaling systems, it was about scaling my soul.

HOW THIS CHAPTER LIVES THE CODE OF HONOR

I build trust – or I build nothing
Some companies faked short-term work to get government support. We didn't – because trust outlasts cash and because people remember who stayed honest when things got tough.

I put people first – always
When the world shut down, we showed up: no panic, no empty promises – just one steady call every morning, with clear communication and full transparency. In a crisis, people don't need perfection – they need presence and consistency.

I innovate for impact
We bet big on adding new optical technologies – and it worked. But the real innovation wasn't the tech: it was the decision to adapt our identity – from inventor to competitor and from disruptor to market leader.

I scale smart and fast
When a competing company blindsided us, we didn't panic. We executed a second-mover strategy, developing Prometheus Panta in 11 months, reclaiming our market, and maintaining our investment in R&D while others cut back.

I build a profitable business that lasts
Operational excellence is not a KPI, it's your cash cow. Reducing our delivery times from seven weeks to 48 hours didn't just impress our customers, it gave us the speed and reputation to be able to scale without fear.

I execute my vision

We shut down entire teams, rebuilt them from scratch, and scaled our operations with discipline. We didn't grow by accident: we built the structure to grow on purpose.

NOW OVER TO YOU

You can't lead a company if you're trapped inside it: step back, step up, and ask the hard questions – especially the ones that hurt your ego. When someone you trust calls you the bottleneck... believe them. When you resist structure... ask what you're afraid of losing. And when your team is waiting... stop giving speeches and start walking the talk.

Because vision without execution is just fantasy – and leadership without transformation is just management in disguise.

CHALLENGE FOR YOU

You say you want to scale, but does your calendar match your vision? Does your organizational chart reflect where you're going or where you've been?

Pick one system – how you run meetings, set goals, or hire leaders. Now redesign it for the company you're becoming, not the one you've already built.

6: THE RISE OF THE HONORABLE ENTREPRENEUR

There wasn't a single moment that gave birth to my belief in the Honorable Entrepreneur. There was no grand event. No dramatic turning point. It was an intense and evolving journey that took place over two decades.

It began in a small Bavarian village, where I felt trapped and restless, searching for a way out. Education and science opened the door, then curiosity pushed me through it. After that, NanoTemper was born: an audacious idea of two inexperienced PhD students that grew into a global business with world-renowned products.

It's been an odyssey full of temptations, failures, and breakthroughs, during which I had to fight for my survival as well as seek personal growth. And now that journey continues beyond the boundaries of NanoTemper: this is the rise of the Honorable Entrepreneur.

Advocating for freedom and independence

We bought back the shares of our Business Angel, who had just turned 80 – a risky age during the pandemic. Volker had served as our White Knight when we needed him the most, back in 2008. He had consistently supported us with his experience whenever we needed it. He didn't ask for extensive reporting – just a few financial numbers and written executive summaries of our products, R&D projects, and overall sales activities. We had always aimed for independence, and the pandemic accelerated our efforts to buy back his shares, while simultaneously motivating him to sell them.

We engaged PwC to produce a fair and transparent valuation of NanoTemper. They decided to use our profitability (EBIT/EBITDA), along with typical transaction multiples from our peer group, to do so. We shared PwC's findings with Volker and made him an offer to buy back his shares based on it. After two rounds of negotiations, we agreed on a sum and a process. We met at the notary's office, signed the contract, then transferred the money. Done! A straightforward, fair, and transparent process – everything went as expected.

After signing the contract and putting down the pen, Volker looked at us and said: "My family is not happy about this. They wanted to keep you as my best asset." This indicated to us even more that we had taken the right step. For Volker, we were entrepreneurs like him who he had wanted to support. For his heirs, however, we would have been just an investment – a number to be increased.

I stepped out of the notary's office. When I took my first breath of fresh air, standing under Munich's blue sky, after two hours of reading through the lengthy transaction contract, a wave of strong emotions hit me – I felt free:

truly free and independent. I felt as though I was being released, now that Stefan and I owned 100% of NanoTemper once more.

Volker was a dream Business Angel: it was always good to have him with us. Yet I still felt that way. For the first time, there was nobody else we had to report to. Nobody else at the backs of our minds when we made decisions or took actions. It was just the two of us, and that feeling of freedom and independence was so strong. This changed something deep inside me and made me ready for something new.

BIG MONEY OR INDEPENDENCE?

In autumn 2021, after an intense US trip that included stops in San Francisco, Philadelphia, and Boston, I returned home with a renewed sense of urgency about NanoTemper's future. Biotech valuations were soaring, and the market was flooded with capital. Stefan and I sat down for one of our long strategic conversations, the kind where nothing is off the table. We considered private equity, tempted by the near-billion-dollar valuations that others were receiving during this pandemic biotech boom.

Our similarly sized competitor, Wyatt Technology, had been acquired by Waters Corporation for 1.4 billion dollars. Finance boutiques estimated our value to be nearer half a billion euros, and private equity and strategic acquirers were constantly approaching us. Now, there was even more money on the table than accompanied the offer we received in March 2019.

However, the thought of giving up control and answering to investors who cared more about returns than vision gave us pause. I realized more than ever that NanoTemper's true strength lay in its independence. We had built a company that thrived on innovation, trust, and long-term thinking – values that often conflicted with the short-term mindsets of financial investors. This decision not only reinforced our commitment to remaining independent, but it also caused me to realize that something is wrong in our startup world.

For decades, founders have been told that "If you want to go fast and big, the only way to go is to seek VC and then private equity," otherwise you'll stay small and meaningless. We have also been told that exiting – selling your company – ought to be the main goal. But our journey with NanoTemper tells a different story. There is another way – the journey that we've taken…

For the first time, I felt an urge to extend my impact beyond NanoTemper. I began building my personal brand on LinkedIn, sharing my experiences, failures, and lessons. The response was and still is overwhelming. What I write there is read more than 3.5 million times per year. I am now connected with thousands of founders and fellow entrepreneurs facing the same struggles that we had to navigate.

Many reach out to me for advice, and I've discovered that I enjoy helping them – I love the fire in their eyes and the energy in our conversations. I started to feel that all my knowledge, my two decades of experience in building and scaling a company, and my ideas could be more beneficial to other founders and entrepreneurs than they would be within NanoTemper. I wanted to guide these people through the challenges of scaling a biotech tools company, helping them to avoid common pitfalls while staying true to their mission. But I realized that in my role as co-CEO of NanoTemper, I just didn't have the time and resources to support as many people as I wanted loved to. So I had to make an important decision…

THE RIGHT TIMING TO RESIGN

How many leaders do you know who resigned from their role at the right time? I think that most of them – such as CEOs, politicians, and even football players and coaches – stay too long. Perhaps Jürgen Klopp, the former German coach of Liverpool FC, had good timing. Maybe Larry Page and Sergey Brin from Google did as well. But generally, staying in power is far too attractive.

Reflecting on these examples, I started contemplating my own role as co-CEO of NanoTemper. Was this the best position for me as a person? Was it the right role for me to contribute effectively to the further growth of NanoTemper?

Whenever I delved deeper into exploring these fundamental questions, something occurred in the organization, pulling me back to the day-to-day business – and stopping my reflections.

Looking back – and being completely honest – I was happy to be distracted from thinking too deeply about my role. It was, as it so often is, much easier to stick to my old behaviors. Why dig deep down when the business is running well enough?

I guess I was afraid of the answers. What if I realized that that I was hindering NanoTemper from growing more strongly by staying in my role as co-CEO? What would I be good for if I resigned – if I renounced all this power and importance?

In June 2024, Stefan and I acknowledged that leading NanoTemper as a "Founders Team" was no longer effective. The structure we had introduced four years earlier had come to its end, as so many previous restructurings had done before. It was slowing us down at a time when our industry was in crisis, with bold – and swift – execution being more important than ever.

We had to spend 10 hours a week coordinating with each other, just to ensure we could present a unified message to our team. We were both frustrated, because neither of us could make decisions independently – and quickly. Something we both need and cherish. Rather, every matter required mutual discussion.

Two conversations catalyzed my understanding of what to do…

Werner, our brilliant Chief Scientific Officer, who was born and raised in South Africa, has a talent of being able to see through things in order to formulate the crucial point. When I discussed our struggles with him, he told me "When two different people talk about the same topic, I still hear two different messages." Those few words thundered around my head. I understood clearly: no matter how much time we spent coordinating, we still weren't being heard as a single voice.

Every month, I meet with Maximilian for lunch. He is the co-founder of the "Internet of Things" company KONUX, which develops sensors for railways. One day, he shared an important piece of wisdom with me: "You must work ON your company, not IN your company." At first, this sounded like another one of those management clichés. But the more I thought about it, the more I realized its truth.

As co-CEO, I'd been deeply involved in the company – caught up in its daily operations, fighting fires, making countless small decisions, and solving urgent problems. It felt like standing in the middle of a dense crowd: I could clearly see the people directly around me, the immediate issues, but I had no idea what was happening beyond – I couldn't see the bigger picture, the trends, or the opportunities lying only a few steps away.

Working on the company means stepping outside of that crowd. It's about finding a vantage point that allows you to see the entire scene. From there, you can shape your long-term strategy, set clear priorities, and steer the direction of your business. You stop reacting to short-term challenges and start proactively creating the future you want – you move from a firefighter mindset to becoming the architect of your own vision.

Both of these conversations, together with my own shifts, made it clear to me that we needed to eliminate the shared leadership of the "Founders Team." But how? We couldn't split NanoTemper into two separate entities. Although that might have been a good solution for us as individuals, it wouldn't necessarily be the best solution for our company.

THE DECISION

At the end of July 2024, we decided that Stefan would become the sole CEO of NanoTemper and that I would step back as co-CEO. This would enable Stefan to execute our strategy as required: swiftly, independently, and taking bold operational decisions – as well as leading with ONE voice.

Resigning as co-CEO was a very tough step for me, which is why it took two years to finally make the decision. In the end, it finally became possible because we found a new role for me: Executive Chairman of NanoTemper.

In this role, I am fully removed from all operations and daily business, allowing me to focus entirely on strategy and on shaping NanoTemper from the outside – to follow the advice to "work ON the company and not IN the company." I continue to serve NanoTemper by acting as its face and voice to the outside world. My responsibilities also include leading our board and overseeing technology transfer and M&A activities.

For me, it's really hard to watch from the outside and not interfere with daily business. Every day, I have to force myself just to listen and not to act. The "just do it" mentality is such a strong part of my personality that just not doing it is the toughest thing I have to face.

After we announced this change, we received feedback from many of our close partners, who said things like "We've never been convinced by this shared co-CEO leadership." Again, it's interesting that you often receive this helpful feedback only after making the change!

Indeed, there were huge advantages to this transition. It freed up my mind. No longer having to battle unpredictable fires, I could extend my impact beyond NanoTemper and finally find the time to listen to the founders and entrepreneurs who kept approaching me. I could discuss their questions and challenges by talking about the tough situations that I'd faced. I felt as though I had created a strong voice inside me – a voice that felt like a call to duty.

That call to duty became something very real at Analytica 2024, which was held in Munich. While chatting casually at the "Innovation in Bavaria" booth, a young man in his mid-twenties wearing a dark gray hoodie approached me, slightly nervously. Shaking my hand, he said softly but earnestly: "Philipp, you probably won't remember me. I heard your keynote at a university workshop in Munich. Because of you, I'm now also in the biotech business."

I stood there, speechless – what a compliment! What a profound moment of realization! My experiences, successes, and failures – especially my failures – could actually inspire others to follow their own entrepreneurial paths.

From that moment on, I knew that my most impactful contribution wouldn't be limited to NanoTemper alone. I'd benefited enormously from the generous mentorship of others. Now, it was my responsibility and my privilege to return the favor, by helping others start, scale, and sustain meaningful ventures of their own.

BECOMING A BUSINESS ANGEL

Over the last few years, during many face-to-face conversations, panel discussions, and conferences, I've noticed a recurring challenge: nearly every founder I've spoken to has struggled to secure funding. Media narratives and startup cultures overwhelmingly promote VC and rapid growth, pushing founders toward valuations in the billions of dollars rather than sustainable businesses that last. And while VC funding can indeed be essential, it's not always the best or only option. Too many founders I've talked to have lost sight of their original vision, their personal life, or even their health, simply because of the pressures that accompany external funding.

Hearing these struggles, I didn't only want to offer advice – I wanted to take concrete action. Because at heart, I'm not just a thinker – I'm a doer. This realization led me to the next stage of my journey: becoming a Business Angel.

In 2008, when NanoTemper was on the brink of collapse, Volker, our Business Angel, changed everything for us. He didn't simply provide us with money: he provided us with belief, freedom, trust, and steady guidance, without ever demanding control or forcing us toward a quick exit. That's exactly the kind of angel investor I aspire to be today.

Inspired by Volker's approach, I now support founders who:

- Are in it for the long term – those who seek to build impactful and enduring businesses rather than seeking quick and shallow wins.
- Have skin in the game – if a founder isn't willing to bet on themselves, why should I?
- Are resourceful and pragmatic – not every startup requires millions in funding from the outset: it's often the case that smart strategic moves and the right early customers can be much more valuable.

I'm not just writing checks, then – I'm actively helping founders negotiate difficult decisions, retain control over their vision, and build something truly meaningful.

So far, I've invested in five remarkable biotech startups, each pioneering bold solutions in healthcare and drug discovery:

1. Opto Biolabs GmbH develops innovative technology to control living organisms with light – led by the driven and energetic Kathrin.
2. Doderm GmbH offers powerful dermatological solutions using antibodies from cow milk, which would otherwise be wasted – Beatrix is an inspiring and integral CEO.
3. Invitris GmbH addresses antimicrobial resistance, one of humanity's greatest health threats, using promising bacteriophage technology – founded by the determined duo Kilian and Patrick.
4. Mallia Therapeutics GmbH is pursuing a revolutionary protein-based hair-loss treatment with billion-dollar potential – guided by exceptional scientific and commercial leadership.
5. Aikium Inc. is pushing the limits of molecule screening and using AI to take risks – it's based in California, with an extraordinarily dedicated founding team.

These founders remind me of myself: driven by purpose and impact, not merely profit. They're not interested in quick exits or fast riches: they aim to build lasting businesses that will genuinely make a difference.

The feedback I receive from these founders confirms my belief:

> *The day you joined Opto Biolabs gave the whole team a boost of energy, confidence, and commitment! It was exactly what we needed. Because you've walked in my shoes, you truly understand our challenges. Your support is always empathetic,*

diplomatic, and deeply respectful. (Kathrin Brenker, Founder and CEO, Opto Biolabs)

Strategic funding, combined with disciplined execution, doesn't just create successful companies – it builds resilient leaders and healthy cultures. It allows founders to remain true to their values, maintain control over their futures, and thrive on their own terms.

It felt good to support five promising startups with energetic and creative founders – and also to mentor many more or even support them via having a role on their board. However, the voice inside me, calling me to duty, continued to be heard. This was a good start – but not good enough. I felt that I had to do something more – something like the next step or level.

THE AWAKENING OF THE HONORABLE ENTREPRENEUR

Every year, hundreds of thousands of startups are founded, across Europe, the US, and beyond. Many of them face the same struggles that we did at NanoTemper in the early days.

Although I was supporting a handful of founders, I still didn't think I was doing enough. With so many of them out there, my impact felt limited. I knew I needed to go beyond what I could do as one person. To do that, I first had to answer some fundamental questions. Who am I now? What is my role? What do I truly stand for?

The answers to those questions started to take shape during a conversation with Daniel, my coach. Daniel had grown up near Hamburg, a city with deep Hanseatic roots, and he's also a history buff, like me. The Hanseatic League once controlled all the trade across the Baltic Sea, being built upon a network of independent merchants who supported one another. These merchants lived by the principle of the "Ehrbarer Kaufmann" – the Honorable Merchant.

One day, Daniel looked at me and said: "What you do, and how you act – it reminds me of an Honorable Merchant."

That struck a chord. I had heard of the concept before, but I returned to it again, with fresh eyes. According to the historical definition, "An Honorable Merchant is guided by a strong sense of responsibility, for their company, society, and the environment. They act with long-term integrity, combining business and ethics into one. They treat their employees fairly, demand excellence, and focus on sustainable value creation."

Reading that, I had one of those rare moments of complete clarity – yes, that's me, that's what I've always tried to be. Building NanoTemper from nothing to more than 56 million euros in revenue, creating jobs, and shaping a culture wasn't just business – it was personal. And it was honorable.

For two years, now, I've shared the idea of the Honorable Merchant on LinkedIn and refined it through hundreds of conversations. Those dialogues have helped me to reimagine the idea for the modern world, giving it a new name: the Honorable Entrepreneur.

This identity took a much longer time to develop, however: 19 years of building NanoTemper, with all the painful mistakes, hard lessons, and challenging the traditional paths we've all been told to follow – especially chasing VC money at all costs or having to play it safe (and slow and small) to avoid failure.

The Honorable Entrepreneur is what finally emerged from that long journey. This identity has many parents and thousands of siblings: you.

Even so, a bigger idea started to take shape: what if NanoTemper's true legacy wasn't just the company, but a community? A movement built on shared principles, with founders supporting one another not only in growing fast, but also in growing with integrity.

That idea wouldn't go away, so I started writing, putting down everything I've learned: the wins, the failures, the hard conversations, and the near-burnouts. What emerged wasn't a rulebook, nor was it a manifesto. Rather, it was a compass – a set of principles to return to when the noise of startup life gets too loud.

Because here's the truth: in a world of pitches, pivots, and pressures, it's easy to forget who you are. I've seen brilliant founders drift – I've been there myself.

That's why I wrote this Code of Honor. Not to impress anyone, but to stay grounded. It's how I make hard decisions and stay aligned with my values. And now, I want to share it with you.

This code is not about perfection: it's about direction and holding steady when everything around us involves noise, speed, and compromise. Let me remind you of the code...

OUR CODE OF HONOR

I build trust – or I build nothing

Trust is the foundation of each and every business. If people can't trust me, they won't follow me. I will communicate openly, act with integrity, and deliver on my commitments: a promise made is a promise kept.

I put people first – always
Business is about people, not just numbers. I will pay good salaries and lead with fairness, loyalty, and respect – empowering my team, valuing diversity, and building a culture where people do their best work. The strongest companies are built by the strongest teams.

I innovate for impact
Innovation isn't about making noise – it's about solving real problems. I won't create technology for the sake of it: I will build solutions that move industries forward, make a difference, and stand the test of time.

I scale smart and fast
Speed wins, but recklessness kills. I will grow with discipline, making bold moves without burning resources or credibility. Scaling is not only about getting bigger, it's also about getting stronger, smarter, and more impactful.

I build a profitable business that lasts
Profitability isn't optional: it's the foundation of long-term success. A strong business is financially independent, sustainable, and built for the future – with more than just selling in mind. I will focus on growth with discipline and resilience.

I execute my vision
Ideas are worthless without action. I won't just talk – I will build, sell, ship, and adapt. I will take bold steps, minimize unnecessary risks, and turn vision into reality – because execution separates the dreamers from the builders.

I give back
Success isn't just about what I build for myself – it's also about how many others I help build. I will mentor, fund, and create opportunities for the next generation of entrepreneurs. A winner takes the prize. A leader passes the torch.

Every entrepreneur faces crossroads – moments when decisions aren't just about strategy, but also about integrity. The Honorable Entrepreneur's Code of Honor is your compass. It will guide you through tough choices, keep you grounded in your values, and ensure that your success isn't just measured by profits, but also by lasting impact.

This is the framework that I try to live by. It's not perfect, but it's the best I've got. And if it resonates with you, then welcome – you're already one of us!

Clarity about who we are must not be the end. Rather, it must be the beginning of a new responsibility: a duty to help others do the same. Because once you find your voice, you start hearing others. And once you find your way, you realize how many are still wandering. That's when a new kind of responsibility begins to take shape: not just to build, but to give back.

That's what happened to me.

Summary

My personal shift moment

In 2024, I didn't just make a career move, I also made a shift in who I am. There were no fireworks – just a slow and often painful realization: it was time to let go.

- I gave up my role as co-CEO. I left the cockpit of NanoTemper so that I could finally work on the company, not in it.

- I turned down private equity and billion-dollar temptations, because freedom and independence meant more to me than valuations.

- I realized that my biggest impact might not come from running a company, but from helping other entrepreneurs to avoid the traps that I had fallen into.

- I stopped defining myself as a "founder" and started living new roles: as mentor, investor, and a voice for a different kind of entrepreneurship.

This was not about growth charts – it was about self-honesty, about making room for others to lead, and about venturing down a path I hadn't seen before.

HOW THIS CHAPTER LIVES THE CODE OF HONOR

I build trust – or I build nothing
Resigning was not only a strategic decision – it was also a trusting move: trusting in Stefan to lead, trusting in our team to rise, and trusting in myself to step away from control without losing purpose.

I build a profitable business that lasts
We bought back our shares, reclaiming 100% ownership and thereby choosing independence over short-term gain. That decision was a love letter to long-term thinking.

I execute my vision
The Honorable Entrepreneur wasn't a brand – it was a calling: forged in failure, rooted in values, and now shared with the founders I support.

I give back
When a young founder thanked me for inspiring his biotech startup, I realized that our lives and the stories that we tell about them have the power to shape others more than we could ever imagine.

NOW OVER TO YOU

This chapter isn't about stepping down – it's about stepping into something bigger.

You don't need a title to lead or an office to make an impact: your real legacy starts when you stop trying to prove yourself and start helping others grow.

That's what being an Honorable Entrepreneur is all about.

CHALLENGE FOR YOU

What's one painful lesson from your journey that someone else needs to hear? And what's one step you can take today to share it?

CODA: LET'S START A MOVEMENT OF HONORABLE ENTREPRENEURS

This book began with a decision: not to sell NanoTemper. But behind that decision lay something deeper: a sense of duty. A duty to my team, to our mission, to our independence, and to the society that made all of this possible.

Every day, founders reach out to me. Some are close to burnout. Others quietly question whether the journey is still worth it. They ask for help, advice, and guidance. I recognize their doubts – I had them too, experiencing the same isolation and the same pressure.

Over time, what began as a few conversations slowly started to become something more: a growing awareness that what I had learned and lived might be of use to others. It became a call to duty.

Not only to help individual founders, but also to offer an alternative vision for entrepreneurship: one that is grounded in long-term responsibility rather than short-term gain, one that values integrity as much as innovation, and one that gives back.

I owe a great deal. I was born into a working-class family in a small village in North Bavaria. There were forests, fields, and a strong sense of belonging in my well-protected childhood, but I also encountered limits. We had very few books at home. I read the Bible twice because it was one of them. It was a peaceful place, but it was also a dead end.

Public education opened the world to me: dedicated teachers, free schools, and a university system that equipped me to go further than I had ever imagined. Without that, NanoTemper wouldn't exist: I simply wouldn't be the entrepreneur I am today.

That's why I believe in giving back: not just in principle, but in practice.

To date, NanoTemper has generated more than 364 million euros in revenue, created more than 250 jobs, and paid 47 million euros in taxes. That money hasn't just vanished into the pockets of a few shareholders: it has returned to the society and the system that shaped me. That's what independence makes possible: not just financial success, but a meaningful contribution.

If you've made it here, I'm guessing that the Code of Honor resonated with you. Maybe, like me, you feel something stirring – a sense that your story doesn't end with your company, but rather that it begins with what you do next.

So here's what I ask of you. If you're still in the grind of building a business, focus on getting to profitability: grow smart, stay in control, build something that lasts, pay your taxes without hiding via loopholes, and contribute to the society that made your path possible.

And once you've made it, give back – mentor other founders and support the next wave of scientists and dreamers.

That's the spirit of the Honorable Entrepreneur.

Because this isn't just about companies: it's about building a legacy you're proud to leave behind and it's about proving that you can do well *and* do good. Staying independent doesn't mean thinking small: it means thinking long term.

This is my call to arms. Let's build a community of founders who share this mindset and dare to do things differently, who help each other to scale fast, smart, and profitably, and who, when they get there, they don't pull the ladder up but lower it back down.

This is the new blueprint: support first, succeed with integrity, then give back freely.

The Honorable Entrepreneur is not just a business model – it's a commitment to you, to your team, and to society.

And if this resonates with you, let's move forward, let's unleash the next generation of entrepreneurs, and let's start a movement – together.

Listen to my podcasts at www.philippbaaske.com or come to one of my keynotes and see me live in action.

Follow me on LinkedIn for more stories and the newest insights: www.linkedin.com/in/philipp-baaske/.

Lead. Live it. The world needs more Honorable Entrepreneurs.

ACKNOWLEDGMENTS

This book isn't just a book – it's half of my life.

The other half comprises the people who carried me through it: sometimes with advice, sometimes with kindness, and often with a well-timed espresso.

To my co-founder, Stefan Duhr – thank you for sharing in the madness of this odyssey, for every late night, every prototype, every turning point, and every time that we dared to do things differently. We've built something rare – and we've remained true to ourselves while doing so.

To the entire NanoTemper team, past and present: you turned vision into reality, you gave your best to something uncertain, and you made the invisible visible. We shared some hard times and great parties together. I've learned more from you than any business book could ever have taught me.

To my mother, whose fight against breast cancer gave me my mission. Herceptin saved your life and changed mine. This company – and this book – started with you.

To my father and brother, the only people in the world who I can sit with for hours on the terrace, saying nothing yet still understanding everything.

To my two wonderful boys, who only know me as part of NanoTemper and are already winning the ping pong matches that are at our social heart.

To my wife, who can see the beauty in the small things: music, art, the Cote d'Azur. You opened up a wonderful new world for me. Naphi Knuske forever.

To Ana Lazic, who told me that I had to write this book – I laughed, but she didn't. It turns out that she saw something I hadn't. Thanks also to Christoph, Karen, and Sam for making this book possible.

To every teacher and professor: don't stop believing! You are shaping our next generation. Education makes THE difference for many.

To the early believers, mentors, customers, and even skeptics – thank you for your questions, your trust, and your challenges. You made us better. And sometimes you even saved us from ourselves.

To the many founders and scientists I've met over the years: this book is my answer to your questions – I wrote it for you, as a testament to the sleepless nights, impossible pivots, and stubborn belief that there's a better way to build.

And, finally, to all my loved ones, who accepted that I can sometimes disappear into my work, yet still chose to stay close to me. I owe you more than I can say.

Danke. Merci. Thank you.

THE AUTHOR

D r. Philipp Baaske co-founded NanoTemper Technologies and now serves as its Chairman. He scaled this Ludwig-Maximilians-University Munich spin-off from a startup founded by two PhD students to a leading – and completely independent – biotech tools company, with revenues of 56 million euros per year and more than 200 employees.

Philipp has authored more than 25 peer-reviewed publications, appearing in *Nature Communications, PNAS*, and other leading journals, and he has been named as co-inventor on 13 patents that established the core technologies behind NanoTemper's instruments.

As well as being included in *CAPITAL* magazine's "Top 40 under 40," Philipp has received Germany's highest founder (Deutscher Gründerpreis) and innovation (Deutscher Innovationspreis) awards. Philipp sits on the Federal Economic Senate (Bundeswirtschaftssenat) of the BWMW e.V., Germany's largest association of small- and medium-sized enterprises, plus he mentors deep-tech startups worldwide.

Cancer in his family first drew him to biotech – *Star Wars* quotations (although he secretly prefers *Star Trek*), dashing to the dance floor when Metallica's "Enter Sandman" plays, and daily long walks along the river Isar keep him grounded.

www.ingramcontent.com/pod-product-compliance
Ingram Content Group UK Ltd.
Pitfield, Milton Keynes, MK11 3LW, UK
UKHW022213270925
463388UK00009B/108